Roadmap
to 5th Grade
Reading:
NORTH CAROLINA EDITION

Roadmap
to 5th Grade
Reading:
NORTH CAROLINA EDITION

by
Stephanie
Reents

Random House, Inc.
New York

www.review.com

This workbook was written by The Princeton Review, the nation's leader in test preparation. The Princeton Review helps millions of students every year prepare for standardized assessments of all kinds. The Princeton Review offers the best way to help students excel on standardized tests.

The Princeton Review is not affiliated with Princeton University or Educational Testing Service.

Princeton Review Publishing, L.L.C.
160 Varick Street, 12th floor
New York, NY 10013

E-mail: comments@review.com

Published in the United States by Random House, Inc., New York.

ISBN 0-375-75578-0

Editor: Russell Kahn
Director of Production: Iam Williams
Design Director: Tina McMaster
Art Director: Neil McMahon
Production Coordinator: Tina McMaster
Production Editor: Kallie Shimek

Manufactured in the United States of America

9 8 7 6 5 4 3 2 1

First Edition

ACKNOWLEDGMENTS

I'd like to thank my editor, Russell Kahn, for his patience and sharp eye.

I'd also like to thank all of the talented and wonderful people at The Princeton Review, including Kristen Azzara, Iam Williams, Mike Rockwitz, Tina McMaster, and Kallie Shimek.

This book is dedicated to H. A. L.

CONTENTS

Parent/Teacher Introduction

About this Book

The Princeton Review is the nation's leader in test preparation. We prepare more than two million students every year with our courses, books, online services, and software programs. In addition to helping North Carolina students with their End-of-Grade (EOG) tests, we coach students around the country on many other statewide standardized tests as well as college-entrance exams such as the SAT-I, SAT-II, PSAT, and ACT. Our strategies and techniques are unique and, most importantly, successful. Our goal is to reinforce skills that students have been taught in the classroom and to show them how to apply these skills to the specific format and structure of the North Carolina EOG Test in Reading Comprehension.

Roadmap to 5th Grade Reading: North Carolina Edition contains three basic elements: lessons, test-preparation practice, and practice tests. Each lesson (or "Mile") focuses on a specific skill such as finding the main idea or supporting details of a passage. They walk students through the basics in ways that emphasize active learning and boil down information into easily retainable (and recallable) chunks. Each lesson is coupled with focused test-prep practice that encourages students to apply what they've just learned. Lastly, the book contains two full-length practice tests. Each test is modeled after the actual EOG Reading Comprehension test in content, format, and style. Having students take our practice tests will familiarize them with the EOG tests, and thus relieve some anxiety when the time comes to take the actual test. This will help you assess which skills students should review and improve upon before they take the EOG Test in Reading Comprehension. It will also show you how much the student has improved after working on the lessons and test-preparation sections in this book. (Answer keys and explanations for the lessons and both practice tests are available beginning on page 167.)

We've also provided a Progress Chart as a way to encourage and motivate students. The Progress Chart is broken up into twenty-two miles (or lessons), and it will help students see how far they've come. Studying for any test can be difficult for young students, and it is as important to encourage good study habits as it is to improve students' weaknesses. Be vigilant about reminding students how well they are doing and how much they've learned. Building confidence goes a long way to help students succeed on any standardized test.

ABOUT THE NORTH CAROLINA END-OF-GRADE READING COMPREHENSION TEST

During the final three weeks of the school year, students will be required to take the state-mandated North Carolina EOG Tests in reading and mathematics. The EOG Test in Reading Comprehension is a 65-question, multiple-choice test. Students are given 115 minutes to read ten passages and to fill in the correct bubbles on an answer sheet provided. (Having students practice by using the answer sheets in this book is a terrific way to help them cut down on bubbling mistakes.) A student's raw score (the number of questions answered correctly) is converted into a developmental score, which is reported in terms of achievement levels. Four achievement levels (I, II, II, and IV) are reported.

Level I: Student does not demonstrate sufficient mastery of knowledge and skills in the subject area to be successful at the next grade level.

Level II: Student demonstrates inconsistent mastery of knowledge and skills in the subject area and is minimally prepared to be successful at the next grade level.

Level III: Student demonstrates mastery of the grade-level subject matter and skills and is well prepared for the next grade level.

Level IV: Student demonstrates an ability to perform in a superior manner clearly beyond that required to be proficient at grade-level work.

Beginning in 2002, test scores will be used to determine student promotion. **Students must achieve at least a Level-III developmental score in both the reading and math tests in order to be promoted to the next grade.** Students will have two opportunities to pass each multiple-choice exam at the end of the school year. Students who do not pass after the second opportunity will be given intervention. This means that those students will either attend summer school and be given a third chance to pass the particular EOG test or they will have to repeat the grade. Students who attend summer school and then fail the EOG test for a third time will still have to repeat the grade.

Students have one chance to be promoted to the next grade even if they fail the EOG test. They may meet with a review panel, and if they can demonstrate the appropriate skills in person, the panel may recommend to the school's principal that the student be promoted. The principal has the ultimate decision on whether to promote a student.

Communicating these stakes to students may be the hardest part of the test-preparation process. It's important to be honest and to remind students that this book covers everything they need to know for the test. The test is just a way for them to show what they know. Keep a positive perspective, and it will help students deal with their testing anxiety.

Before students begin their test preparation, take a moment to review the table of contents in the book. We've tried to present the material in a way that each skill presented builds on the previous one, but we realize that every student and every class has different strengths and weaknesses. There's no harm if students work on the lessons out of sequence; individual students have individual test-preparation needs.

STUDENT INTRODUCTION

ABOUT THIS BOOK

We're guessing that you don't like tests. Given the choice, you'd never take another test again, right? And a book all about tests—what could be worse than that! Well, the *Roadmap to 5th Grade Reading: North Carolina Edition* makes it fun to learn how to take tests. The book includes games to play, puzzles to finish, pictures to draw, and questions to answer.

Every lesson in this book is another "mile" on a trip that ends with you doing your best on the North Carolina End-of-Grade (EOG) Test in Reading. Each mile reviews a skill that you'll be tested on. We'll take you step-by-step through all the basics. And after you review, you get a chance to show what you know. What could be more fun than that! Track yourself on the Progress Chart in the beginning of the book by coloring in every mile after you've finished it.

In no time flat, you'll be an expert at reading. The only thing left will be to show your parents and teachers what you've learned by acing your EOG test. And just in case you're worried about how well you do, we've given you two complete practice tests. These practice tests can show you exactly how great your reading skills are!

You still might not like tests. That's okay. But by the time you get to the end of the *Roadmap to 5th Grade Reading,* you'll be ready to do your best on them!

WHAT ELSE CAN I DO?

There are other things you can do to prepare for the North Carolina EOG Test in Reading. You should

- **Ask questions.** If you are confused after you finish a mile (or even just one question), ask a parent or teacher for help. Asking questions is the best way to make you understand what you have to do to do your best!

- **Read.** Read everything you can. Read the newspaper, magazines, books, plays, poems, comics, the back of your cereal box. The more you read, the better you read. And the better you read, the more likely you are to do well on the EOG reading test.

- **Learn new words.** Vocabulary is a big part of this test. The more words you know, the easier the test will seem. Try carrying index cards with you. Any time you come across a word you don't know, write it down. When you have time, look up the definition and write it on the back of the card. You can turn learning vocabulary into a game. Use your cards to test yourself. Set goals for learning new words every week. Ask teachers for help if you want. I bet they can suggest some great new words to learn.

- **Eat well and get a good night's sleep.** Your brain is part of your body. Your body doesn't work well when you don't eat good food and get enough sleep. Neither does your brain. On the night before the test, make sure you go to bed at your normal time. You should also have a healthy breakfast on the morning of the test day. Nothing will help you do better than being awake and alert while you are taking your EOG reading test.

This is just the beginning of the road. There are great things to learn ahead. So buckle your seatbelt and get ready to take off down the first mile to reading excellence.

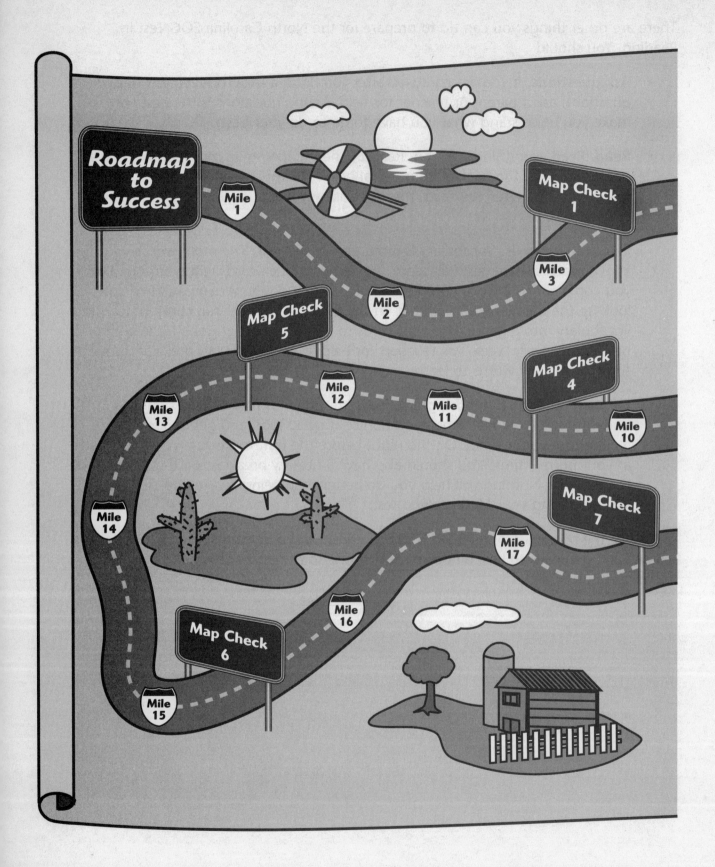

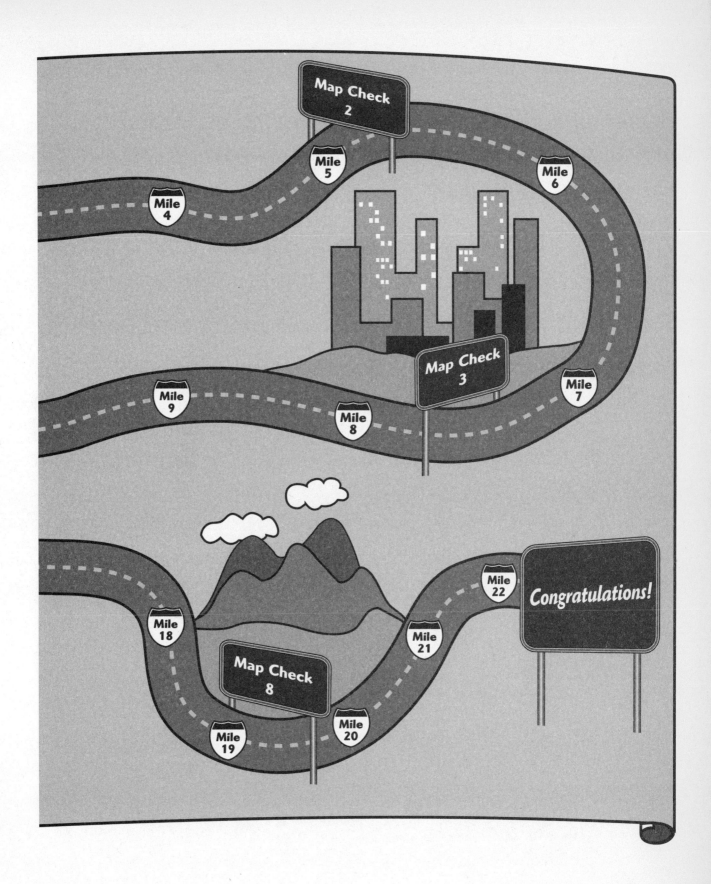

MILE-BY-MILE

10

Before setting off on an adventure, you usually consult a map. A map helps you figure out where you are going and how you're going to get there. Just like using a map for traveling, before you begin to read a book, you can look at its cover, read its title, and scan its pages to find out about the book and its contents. Predicting a book's subject matter will make reading it easier—because you'll know where you're headed.

Directions: Look at the book covers below. Based on the titles, write down what kinds of information or stories you would expect to read in each book. One example has been done for you.

How the Kangaroo Got Its Pouch and Other Animal Stories

A. _Stories_
   about animals

North Carolina Bus Schedule

B. _____

Eyewitness Accounts of the Eruption of Mt. St. Helens

C. _____

Birthday Party Skits

D. _____

Great Scientific Discoveries

E. _____

At the Zoo and Other Poems

F. _____

Exploring Florida

G. _____

Young Chess Champions

H. _____

Eliza and Her Imaginary Friend

I. _____

Treasures from the Ocean

J. _____

Nursery Rhymes from Around the World

K. _____

Making Beads and Other Craft Projects

L. _____

Read the titles of the two books that appear below. One book is fiction, and the other book is nonfiction. Identify the books by writing "Fiction" or "Nonfiction" next to the books. Then read the sentences below the books. Some sentences came from the fiction book, and some came from the nonfiction book. On the line next to each sentence, write "Fiction" or "Nonfiction."

 _____    _____

1.   One kind of fish called shad has 769 bones. _____

2.   Fish can swallow people if they get angry. _____

3.   Eric the Elephant can play songs with his trunk. _____

4.   A black bear carried off a small child and raised him as a cub. _____

5.   A snail can lay up to eighty-five eggs at a time. _____

6.   Cats from Prussia can live to be one hundred years old if they don't smoke. _____

7.   The Komodo dragon is the world's largest lizard. _____

8.   Elephants are born with large ears so they can fly. _____

9.   Porcupine quills are about 7.5 centimeters long. _____

10. A pack of rabid dogs took over half of Winston-Salem. _____

Write one more statement that you would expect to find in _Amazing Animal Facts_.

11. _____

Write one more statement that you might find in _Fantastic Animal Stories_.

12. _____

MILE 2: WHY DO PEOPLE READ?

People read for many different reasons. There are probably three major reasons a person would read something.

- People read to have fun.

- People read to gain knowledge.

- People read to learn how to do things.

Directions: Look at the different types of subjects below. Each example shows a different type of writing. On the next page are the three different reasons people read. Write the name of each kind of reading selection under the column that best describes why someone would read it. Cross out the book after you have written your answer. You should do this to make sure you don't write the same book twice. The first example has been done for you.

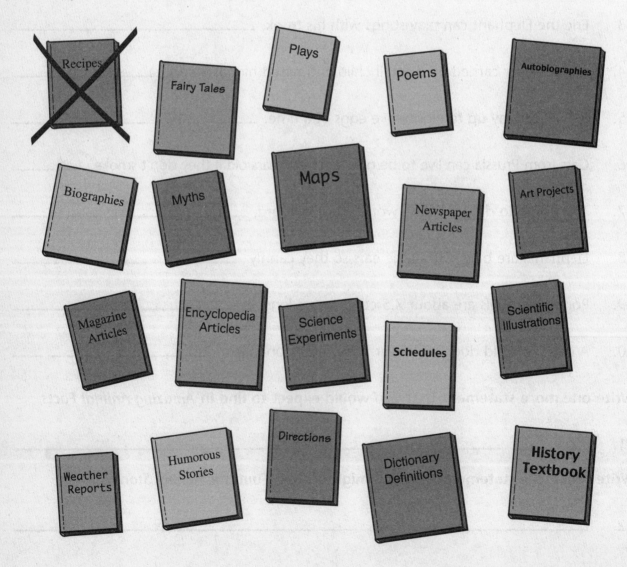

Mile 2: Why Do People Read?

Keep in mind that the answers aren't set in stone. For example, people read newspapers primarily to gain information, but they also may read them to have fun.

To have fun	To gain knowledge	To learn how to do things
		Recipes
_____	_____	_____
_____	_____	_____
_____	_____	_____
_____	_____	_____
_____	_____	_____
_____	_____	_____

Directions: The words in the box below list five different types of reading selections. Over the next two pages, read each of the short selections. Use the words from the box to complete the sentences that follow each selection. Then, answer the question.

Poem

Encyclopedia article

Story

Schedule

History book

Mohandas Gandhi taught people to use a peaceful approach to change things they didn't like about the world. He began developing his philosophy during the years that he lived in South Africa. There, he realized that Indians did not have the same rights as white South African citizens. Gandhi began working to help Indians gain equal rights. Although he was arrested many times, he never used violence in his protests.

1. This reading selection is from _____.

2. Why would somebody read this selection? _____

    _____

    _____

Raleigh to Chapel Hill

Bus #	Depart	Arrive
125	6:00 A.M.	8:00 A.M.
150	9:00 A.M.	11:00 A.M.
175	12:00 P.M.	2:00 P.M.
200	3:30 P.M.	5:30 P.M.
225	8:15 P.M.	10:15 P.M.

3. This reading selection is from _____.

4. Why would somebody read this selection? _____

    _____

    _____

Mile 2: Why Do People Read?

For hundreds of years, explorers have written and drawn treasure maps—detailed directions that will supposedly lead to riches. One of the most famous treasure maps leads to Cocos Island off the coast of Costa Rica. In the nineteenth century, a Scottish captain named William Thompson stole tons of gold, jewels, and other treasures from Peru and hid them on the island. He never returned for the treasure, but he gave a treasure map to his friend John Keating just before he died. Keating and hundreds of others have searched for the hidden riches, but none of them has had any luck. Perhaps, it is still hidden on Cocos Island.

5. This reading selection is from _____.

6. Why would somebody read this selection? _____

_____

It rained and rained and rained some more
We were scared to go outdoors
Water filled the streets and lawns
The puddles were as big as ponds
It rained all night and rained all morn
It was a never-ending storm
It rained at lunch and supper too
It rained so much, there was nothing to do.

7. This reading selection is from _____.

8. Why would somebody read this selection? _____

_____

Min heard the door open, then the sound of someone tiptoeing downstairs. An owl called out, and Min shivered underneath her covers. It had been a strange day, beginning with the bottle she'd found on the beach. Tucked inside was a note written in an unknown language; something about the way it was written—with shaky handwriting in red ink—told Min that the message was important.

9. This reading selection is from _____.

10. Why would somebody read this selection?_____

_____

MILE 3: HOW DO PEOPLE READ?

Directions: Your teacher has given you a reading assignment for homework. The seven steps you should take for reading this assignment are listed below, but they are out of order. On the next page, write the steps in the best order. The first step has been done for you.

- Think about and summarize what you've read.

- Read the selection.

- Read the titles and headings in the assignment.

- Use the dictionary, the library, or the Internet to learn more about what you've read.

- Decide the purpose of the reading assignment.

- Go to a quiet, comfortable place to read.

- Reread the parts of the assignment that you had trouble with and use context clues to figure them out.

1. *Go to a quiet, comfortable place to read.*
_____

2. _____
_____

3. _____
_____

4. _____
_____

5. _____
_____

6. _____
_____

7. _____
_____

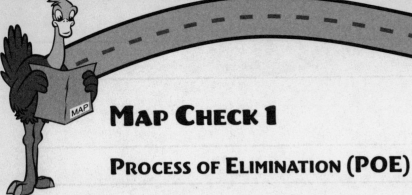

MAP CHECK 1

PROCESS OF ELIMINATION (POE)

It's time to take a break from your journey and review an important test-taking strategy. Sometimes you might not know the best answer to a question on a North Carolina EOG Test. Don't worry. You can use Process of Elimination (POE) to help you find the best answer. It's easy. First, rule out the choices that you know are wrong. Then, choose the best answer from the remaining choices. You might still have to guess, but you'll increase your chances of guessing correctly if you have eliminated several choices. Let's look at an example.

▶ Which of the following did Snow White's evil stepmother use to poison Snow White?

A   ice cream

B   the prince

C   an apple

D   a wood cabin

Step 1   Using POE, you should look at each answer choice and ask yourself, "Is this answer choice *right* or *wrong*?" Let's get started. Is answer choice (A) correct?

☐ Yes, it is correct. But I'll read the other answer choices just in case.

☐ No, it is not correct because _____

Eliminate it.

☐ I don't know. I'll keep it and read the other answer choices.

If you're not sure how the stepmother poisoned Snow White, you might skip (A).

Step 2   Is answer choice (B) correct?

☐ Yes, it is correct. But I'll read the other answer choices just in case.

☐ No, it is not correct because _____

Eliminate it.

☐ I don't know. I'll keep it and read the other answer choices.

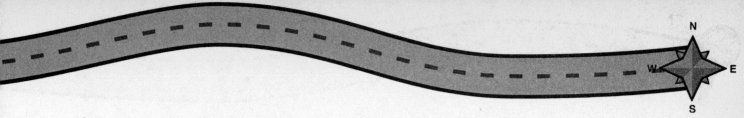

If you remember that the prince was a *good* character in the story of Snow White, you can use POE to get rid of this answer choice.

Step 3 Is answer choice (C) correct?

☐ Yes, it is correct. But I'll read the other answer choices just in case.

☐ No, it is not correct because _____
Eliminate it.

☐ I don't know. I'll keep it and read the other answer choices.

If you think the stepmother poisoned Snow White with an apple, hold on to this choice. Then check the other answer choices.

Step 4 Is answer choice (D) correct?

☐ Yes, it is correct. But I'll read the other answer choices just in case.

☐ No, it is not correct because _____
Eliminate it.

☐ I don't know. I'll keep it and read the other answer choices.

How could the stepmother have poisoned Snow White with a wood cabin? It seems unlikely, so you can get rid of (D).

Step 5 Which of the answer choices remain? _____

If you have more than one answer choice remaining, you must make your best guess. Even though you're guessing, you increase the chance that you'll guess correctly if you eliminate even one wrong answer choice. Usually one answer choice is definitely wrong.

In this case, you could probably use POE to get rid of (B) and (D), even if you weren't sure how Snow White was poisoned. That leaves (A) and (C) as possible choices. The answer is (C).

Even if you think the first answer choice is correct, be sure to read *every* answer choice before choosing a final response. You might find a better answer if you continue reading the other choices.

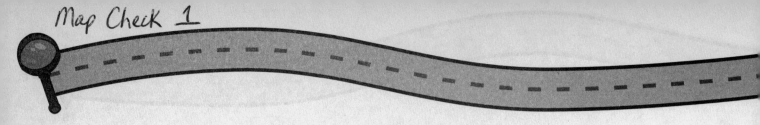

Sally Ride, the First American Woman in Space

Sally Ride was the first American female to fly in space. Born in 1951 in Encino, California, Ride graduated from Stanford University. During college, Ride decided that she wanted to be an astronaut.

Ride began training in 1978. Out of thirty-four astronauts in training, only six were women. Ride says all of the astronauts treated one another with respect: "The men in that group were very supportive and considered us as equals."

Astronaut training was very challenging. Ride had to become an expert on every detail of the space shuttle. "[I]t's a lot like being in school in a very difficult course," she said, "where you have to master everything."

Before going into space, Ride worked as part of the support crew for other shuttle voyages. She got her chance to go into space in 1983 on the space shuttle *Challenger*. The shuttle took off from Florida. It stayed in orbit for 147 hours and landed in California.

Ride served as flight engineer on her first shuttle ride. Along with two other astronauts, she helped to launch and land the shuttle. She was also responsible for operating the shuttle's robot arm. "The way you work the robot arm," Ride explained, "is by using two hand controllers: One moves the arm up and down and to the side; and the other rotates it."

Ride said the take-off was more exciting than the landing. "Lift-off is very exciting!" she said. "There isn't really time to be scared, but it's exhilarating and sometimes overwhelming."

She was very lucky because she didn't get sick in space. About half of the astronauts do get sick, Ride said. "The good news is that they all report that it goes away in a day or two, and then they feel fine for the rest of the mission."

Ride is currently a physics professor at the University of California, San Diego. She encourages all her students to consider studying science. "Whether it's as an astronaut or an engineer in mission control or a scientist receiving data from Mars, there are lots of exciting possibilities," she said. "The most important thing is to get a good background in science while you're in school."

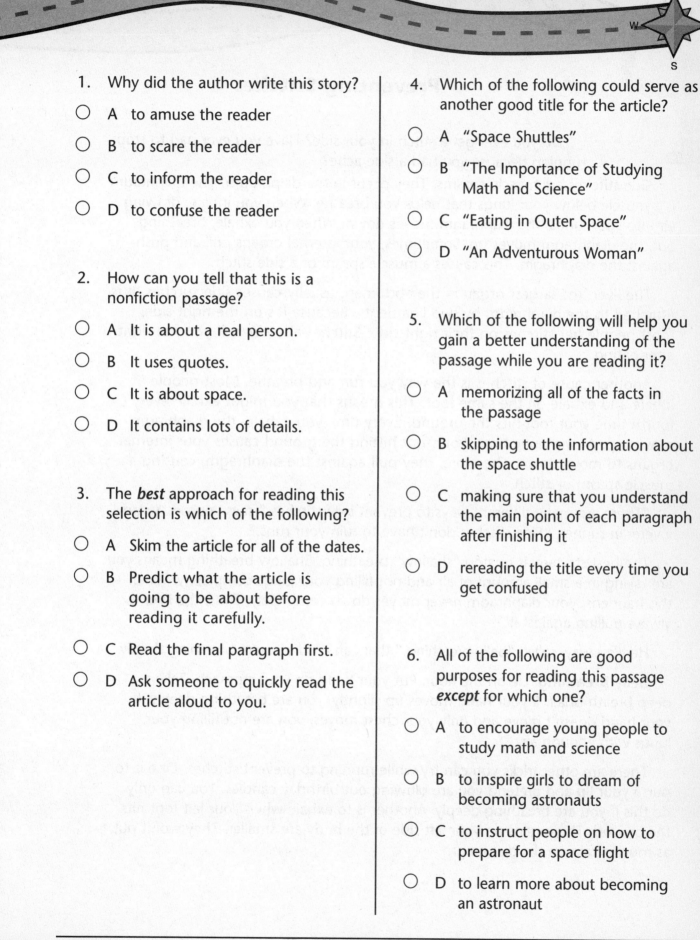

1. Why did the author write this story?

   ○ A to amuse the reader

   ○ B to scare the reader

   ○ C to inform the reader

   ○ D to confuse the reader

2. How can you tell that this is a nonfiction passage?

   ○ A It is about a real person.

   ○ B It uses quotes.

   ○ C It is about space.

   ○ D It contains lots of details.

3. The *best* approach for reading this selection is which of the following?

   ○ A Skim the article for all of the dates.

   ○ B Predict what the article is going to be about before reading it carefully.

   ○ C Read the final paragraph first.

   ○ D Ask someone to quickly read the article aloud to you.

4. Which of the following could serve as another good title for the article?

   ○ A "Space Shuttles"

   ○ B "The Importance of Studying Math and Science"

   ○ C "Eating in Outer Space"

   ○ D "An Adventurous Woman"

5. Which of the following will help you gain a better understanding of the passage while you are reading it?

   ○ A memorizing all of the facts in the passage

   ○ B skipping to the information about the space shuttle

   ○ C making sure that you understand the main point of each paragraph after finishing it

   ○ D rereading the title every time you get confused

6. All of the following are good purposes for reading this passage *except* for which one?

   ○ A to encourage young people to study math and science

   ○ B to inspire girls to dream of becoming astronauts

   ○ C to instruct people on how to prepare for a space flight

   ○ D to learn more about becoming an astronaut

Preventing Stitches

Do you ever get a stitch in your side? Have you ever had to stop running because you had a side ache?

Side stitches are muscle spasms. They occur in the diaphragm. The diaphragm is a muscle below your lungs that helps you breathe. When you inhale, drawing air into your lungs, the diaphragm moves down. When you exhale, breathing out, the diaphragm moves up. Sometimes, your internal organs pull and push against the diaphragm. This causes a muscle spasm or a side stitch.

The liver, the largest organ in the abdomen, usually causes side stitches. It is attached to the diaphragm by two ligaments. Because it's on the right side, most people get stitches on their right side. Stitches also occur if you run right after eating.

Another cause of stitches is the way you run and breathe. Most people inhale and exhale on the same foot. This means that you might exhale every fourth time your foot hits the ground. Every time you exhale, the diaphragm moves up. At the same time, your foot hitting the ground causes your internal organs to move down. Therefore, they pull against the diaphragm, causing a muscle spasm or stitch.

"There are many different ways to prevent side stitches," says Lourdes Santos, a veteran runner. "Side stitches don't have to ruin your runs."

The best strategy is to stop "shallow" breathing. Shallow breathing means you are taking in a small amount of air and not filling your lungs completely. When this happens, your diaphragm never moves down completely. Thus, the liver is always pulling against it.

Here's a way, called "belly breathing," that can ensure you're breathing deeply.

Belly Breathing: Lie on the floor. Put your hand on your stomach. Take a deep breath of air. If your hand moves up slightly, you are breathing deeply. If your hand doesn't move and only your chest moves, you are not filling your lungs with enough air.

There are other tricks you can try while running to prevent stitches. One is to purse your lip and pretend you are blowing out birthday candles. You can only do this if you are breathing deeply. Another is to exhale when your left foot hits the ground. The organs on your left side of the body are smaller. They won't put as much strain on the diaphragm.

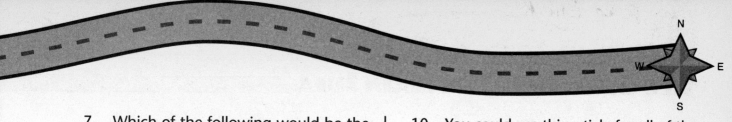

7. Which of the following would be the *best* way to read and understand the information presented in this article?

   ○ A Read the title and final paragraph.

   ○ B Read the example about belly breathing first.

   ○ C After reading each paragraph, jot down a few words summarizing its main idea.

   ○ D Scan the article for difficult words and look them up before beginning to read.

8. Which of the following *best* describes the purpose of this article?

   ○ A to instruct

   ○ B to mystify

   ○ C to entertain

   ○ D to analyze

9. Which is the *first* thing you should do if you don't understand the meaning of the word "exhale"?

   ○ A Circle the word.

   ○ B Look up the word in the encyclopedia.

   ○ C Reread the section where it appears for context clues.

   ○ D Look up the word in the dictionary.

10. You could use this article for all of the following purposes *except* for which?

    ○ A to teach people how to prevent side stitches

    ○ B to explain how side stitches occur

    ○ C to teach people how to run faster

    ○ D to encourage people to breathe more deeply when exercising

11. Into which of the following categories does this passage *best* fit?

    ○ A nonfiction article

    ○ B recipe

    ○ C autobiography

    ○ D story

12. Which of the following would be an equally good title for this passage?

    ○ A "Belly Breathing"

    ○ B "The Largest Organ in the Abdomen"

    ○ C "Running and Breathing"

    ○ D "Sideaches: What They Are and How to Get Rid of Them"

MILE 4: FINDING THE MAIN IDEA

The last time you returned from a vacation, your friends may have asked you, "What did you do on your trip?" Instead of telling them about every little thing, you probably told them about the highlights or the main events of your vacation. Well, some questions in school or on EOG tests may ask you to identify the main idea of fiction and nonfiction selections. Your job will be to figure out what the selection was mainly about.

In nonfiction passages, the main idea often comes in the first paragraph, and it describes the overall ideas presented in the article. For fiction passages, the main idea is usually what the main character (or you) learned from the story.

Directions: Read the four passages over the next two pages. After each one, write its main idea.

Dom woke to the sound of rustling outside his bedroom door. He looked at the clock. It was 11:15 A.M. How could he have slept so late? He jumped out of bed and rushed into the kitchen.

His sister was putting away the waffle iron. "Hi, sleepyhead," she said.

Dom gulped, "Are there any more waffles?"

"No," his sister replied. "We finished breakfast an hour ago."

Dom's stomach rumbled, and a frown spread across his face. His sister must have noticed his expression. "I guess you'll have to have cold cereal for breakfast," she said.

As Dom poured a bowl of cornflakes, he vowed to get up extra early the next day.

1. What is the main idea of this passage? _____

_____

There are several different reasons that oceans are salty and rivers are not. Oceans are fed by rivers. As rivers travel to oceans, they collect salt and minerals from the rocks and sand at the bottom of the riverbeds. Rivers don't taste salty, however, because they are constantly receiving fresh water from sources like rain and natural springs.

In contrast, oceans fill with river water. This water is filled with all of the salt and minerals collected by the rivers. In addition, the ocean floor also contains minerals that dissolve in the water. Both of these make oceans salty.

2. What is the main idea of this passage? _____

_____

Juanita was daydreaming about the new rollerblades she had received that morning for her birthday when she suddenly noticed her class was lining up.

"What's going on?" she whispered to her friend Susan.

"There's a special assembly," Susan replied with a mysterious smile. "Didn't you hear what Mrs. Hornsby said?"

Juanita felt confused. "Juanita," Mrs. Hornsby said. "I need to talk to you in the hallway." Juanita was sure she was in boiling water with Mrs. Hornsby.

"No daydreaming!" Mrs. Hornsby said with a scowl on her face. Juanita walked into library with her head hung low.

"Surprise!" her friends shouted. "Happy birthday!"

3. What is the main idea of this passage? _____

   _____

Dehydration is a common problem. When you're dehydrated it means that your body has lost or used more fluids than it has taken in. You lose fluids in lots of ordinary ways—by sweating, by going to the bathroom, and even by breathing.

There are many different ways our bodies tell us they need more fluids. Being thirsty is one sign. Feeling very tired even though you are getting a lot of sleep is another. Only going to the bathroom once or twice a day is another indication that you're dehydrated.

Because our bodies need water to stay healthy, pay attention to these signs and pour yourself a big glass of water.

4. What is the main idea of this passage? _____

   _____

Directions: Read the passage below and answer the questions that follow.

Frederick Douglass

The famous author and champion of the rights of African Americans and women traveled a long way from his humble beginnings. Frederick Douglass was born in Tuckahoe, Maryland, in 1817 or 1818. He didn't know his exact birthday or even how old he was. He never met his father, although he knew he was a white man, and he was separated from his mother when he was just seven years old. As a slave, Douglass had few rights.

Life was difficult for slaves. Their masters made them work hard and gave them little in return. Each month, a slave usually received a small amount of food: eight pounds of pork or fish and one bushel of cornmeal. Each year, their masters gave them two shirts, a pair of pants, a pair of stockings, and one pair of shoes. Children who were slaves received even less.

Douglass began working when he was just a small boy. Because he was too young to work in the fields, he did odd jobs around his master's house. Before Douglass was nine years old, his master sent him to Baltimore to work for some relatives.

This was a turning point for him. The wife of his new master, Mrs. Auld, liked the young boy and began teaching him to read. However, when her husband found out about the lessons, he put a stop to them. It was against state law to teach him how to read! Douglass, however, was determined to learn more. He befriended some white boys who taught him what they were learning in school.

As Douglass became more educated, he realized he was a slave, which meant he would be enslaved for life. Knowing this, he continued to study, with the goal of finding a way to gain his freedom.

Douglass began plotting ways to escape slavery. He saved the pennies that his master gave him, and finally in 1838, he escaped to New York, a free state where slavery was illegal. Douglass was terrified that he would be caught and returned to his master. He worked hard, setting aside his earnings. Eventually, he saved $700. He used this money to pay his master and buy his freedom.

Having gained his freedom, Douglass used his gift for writing to persuade others to abolish slavery. He wrote three autobiographies about his struggles to escape his fate as a slave. He also published and edited a newspaper called *The North Star*, which called for the end of slavery.

Frederick Douglass's books and speeches in the 1800s helped support the Blacks' rights movement. After the Civil War, Congress passed the Fourteenth Amendment to the Constitution ensuring some guaranteed rigths to Blacks. Douglass also helped convince voters to vote for Ulysses S. Grant in the 1868 presidential election. With Grant's victory, the Fifteenth Amendment was passed, allowing all citizens the right to vote, regardless of race.

5. Write a summary of this passage.

  _____

  _____

  _____

  _____

  _____

6. Find the sentence or phrase from the passage that most clearly states the main idea.
    Write it here.

  _____

  _____

  _____

  _____

MILE 5: FINDING SUPPORTING IDEAS

Now that you've practiced finding the main idea, learn how to answer supporting idea questions. Supporting ideas are statements or sentences that help you draw a conclusion. Pretend you wake up one morning and look out the window. The sky is clear. Birds are chirping. The sun is peeking over the hills in the distance. You'd probably say to yourself, "It's going to be a beautiful day." You'd draw this conclusion based on the things (the sky, the birds, the sun) that you observed. These are supporting details.

Directions: Read the following story. On the page that follows, write the main idea of the story in the central circle of the diagram. Write the supporting ideas that support the story's main idea in the squares around the circle.

Kayaking

Last weekend, I went on a three-day kayaking trip led by two guides through the San Juan Islands. Kayaking is a very challenging activity.

We started our adventure at Andrews Bay on the west side of San Juan Island. First, we had to carry the kayaks to the edge of the beach. Because they were double kayaks—which means they hold two people—they were very heavy to carry. They got even heavier after we loaded them up with food and camping gear.

Packing them was difficult because all of our supplies and equipment had to fit into small storage bins in the front and back of the kayak. While I was trying to stuff my sleeping bag, tent, and dry bag (a waterproof bag that kept my clothes dry) into the front storage bin, I bruised my thumb. Ow!

After the guides gave us a quick lesson on paddling, we climbed into the boats. We were all wearing kayaking skirts that looked like rubber overalls with skirts. We attached the bottom of the skirts to a lip around the kayak opening in which we sat. This kept water from splashing into the kayaks. I had trouble attaching my kayaking skirt, but the guide came and helped me.

Kayaks are steered using rudders. The person sitting in the back controls the rudder with two foot pedals. Pushing on the pedals makes the kayak go left or right. It takes a while to get the hang of steering. For the first mile or two, we zigzagged back and forth. This, of course, made our journey longer and more tiring.

I thought kayaking would be easy because I have canoed a lot. Boy, was I wrong! Canoe paddles have a blade on one end; kayak paddles have blades on both ends. Kayaking is like pedaling a bike with your arms. You push the left blade into the water, then the right blade. The guides told us that it was important to push the paddle, rather than pulling it. I guess I was doing it incorrectly because my neck and arms got sore.

Once I finally started paddling correctly, we came to one of the most difficult parts of the trip: crossing Spieden Channel. Although the currents were flowing with us, the wind was blowing against us. It took us two hours to paddle six miles. Our kayak rocked up and down in the waves. Several times I ended up with a mouthful of seawater!

You can't imagine how happy I was when we paddled toward the campground on Stuart Island. But after drinking my first cup of hot chocolate, I started growing excited about the next day's kayaking challenges.

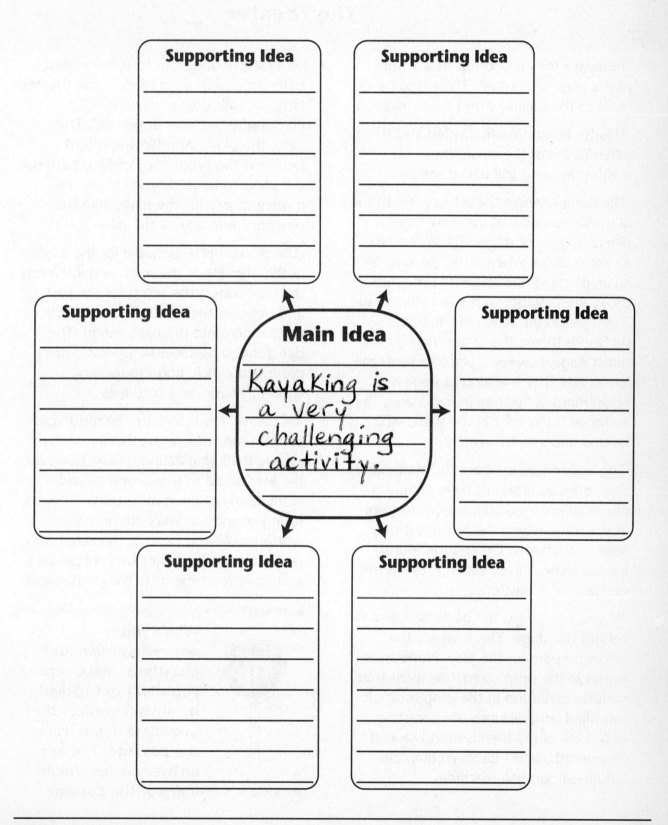

Main Idea

Kayaking is a very challenging activity.

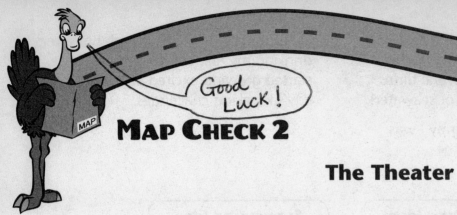

MAP CHECK 2

The Theater

Today we took a field trip to a theater where plays are put on. There is so much more to the theater than I ever imagined.

Theater buildings are divided into three different areas: the stage, the auditorium, and the backstage area.

The stage is where the actors perform the play. We learned that there are three different types of stages. The oldest type is an arena stage. When actors perform on an arena stage, the audience surrounds them. Arena stages were used more than 2,000 years ago. When the audience surrounds three sides of the stage it is a thrust stage. Scenery is placed against the fourth side. The final kind of stage is a proscenium or "picture frame" stage. The audience sits in front of the stage, which is located underneath an arch.

The auditorium is where the audience sits. Some auditoriums have orchestra pits, a submerged area directly in front of the stage where the musicians play their instruments. Other auditoriums have a second level, which is called the mezzanine or balcony.

As you can guess, the backstage area is behind the stage. This is where the actors prepare for the play. Props are stored in the prop room. We spent thirty minutes exploring in the prop room. It was filled with all kinds of interesting stuff. One of my friends found several fake swords, and I discovered an old-fashioned gumball machine.

After we finished our tour, we visited different people who work in the theater. First, we talked to a playwright. Playwrights are very important. They write the plays. Another important person is the producer. Producers choose the plays to be performed, raise the money to pay for the plays, hire the directors, and pay all the bills.

The director is responsible for the quality of the play. He or she reads and interprets the play, selects the actors for the parts, and oversees the transformation of the written play into dramatic action. The director also oversees all aspects of the production, including the scenery, lighting, music, and costumes.

Of course, the actors are the most visible people who work in the theater. Many people think that acting is easy. However, the actors told us that acting is hard work. Many of them have acted for years, taking courses on voice (to pronounce words loudly and clearly), characterization (to understand different kinds of people), and body movement (to move on stage).

Tip

When you're answering main idea questions, make sure you don't get tricked by answer choices that provide a detail from the passage. The best answer choice should provide a summary of the passage.

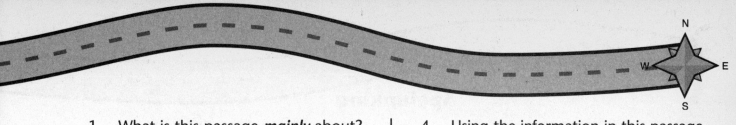

1. What is this passage *mainly* about?

   ○ A Many different people are involved in putting on plays.

   ○ B Scenery, lighting, music, and costumes are important in plays.

   ○ C Actors must go to school to learn how to act.

   ○ D Playwrights have very important jobs.

2. Putting on a play involves doing all of the following things *except* for which one?

   ○ A transforming writing into dramatic action

   ○ B hiring a director

   ○ C holding auditions to find the right actors

   ○ D selling refreshments during intermission.

3. Which question would you have trouble answering based on the passage?

   Tricky! Be careful!

   ○ A What is a producer's primary responsibility?

   ○ B Who hires the actors?

   ○ C How do voice lessons help actors?

   ○ D How long does it take to prepare for a play?

4. Using the information in this passage, you would be *most likely* to complete which of the following reports?

   ○ A Writing Novels

   ○ B American Directors

   ○ C Theater Arts

   ○ D Famous Actors

5. How are the jobs of producers and directors similar?

   ○ A Both involve raising money for the production.

   ○ B Both include acting in the theater.

   ○ C Both involve overseeing the work of actors.

   ○ D Both have many responsibilities.

6. Taking a field trip to a theater *most likely* teaches students which of the following lessons?

   ○ A the excitement of rehearsals

   ○ B the complexity of putting on plays

   ○ C the glamour of the director of the theater

   ○ D the importance of the actors

   Concentrate!

Spelunking

1   When Daniel and Lydia ducked into the entrance of the cavern, they didn't know what to expect. They were on a spelunking expedition with Lydia's father. Spelunkers are people who explore caverns and caves. It's an exciting hobby that takes people to unexplored or out-of-the-way places.

2   "It's time to turn on your miner's headlamp," Lydia's father said.

3   "Today we're going to be exploring a cavern," Lydia's father said. "I want to show you and your friend how much fun caves can be."

4   "What's the difference between a cavern and a cave?" Daniel asked.

5   "Great question," Lydia's father said as they put on their gloves and kneepads to protect themselves from getting any scrapes. "A cave can be any hollowed out area on the side of a hill or in the ground. A cavern is a very large cave. Usually a cavern has at least one huge room. That's what we will be looking for today."

6   The three began walking down a dark tunnel. Their headlamps provided just enough light for them to see the way. Caverns are generally found in places where there are large deposits of limestone. Limestone is a soft rock. It is made from the ancient remains of coral, mollusks, plankton, and other marine organisms. When water with small traces of carbonic acids falls on limestone, it begins to dissolve the rock by trickling into cracks and crevices. Over long periods of time, these cracks and crevices become larger. Eventually, they become larger cavities and caverns.

7   The three spelunkers knew that the cave had once been filled with water. However, as the climate grew drier, the water disappeared. Almost!

8   "Hey, I think I just stepped in a puddle!" Lydia squealed. She shined her flashlight down at the floor. They had turned a corner, and a small stream was running along the bottom of the passageway. It's not uncommon to find streams in caves. Some caves even boast underground lakes.

9   Suddenly, Lydia's father stopped. "I can't believe it," he said excitedly.

10 Up ahead was a huge cavern with a fifteen-foot-high ceiling. Hanging from the ceiling were beautiful formations that looked like icicles. Of course, they weren't really icicles. They were actually stalactites. Stalactites form when water drips from a cave's ceiling. Each drop of water leaves behind a hard substance called calcite. Eventually, the calcite starts to look like a giant icicle.

11 Lydia shined her flashlight on the ground. "Look," she cried, "there are stalactites on the floor also."

12 Lydia's father shook his head, "Not quite. The structures growing from the floor are called stalagmites. Sometimes, stalagmites and stalactites join and form columns. Do either of you see any here?"

13 Daniel's flashlight traveled around the room. "Is that one?" Illuminated by the light were three rock columns.

14 "Yep!" Lydia's father's voice echoed in the cavern. "This place is a goldmine!"

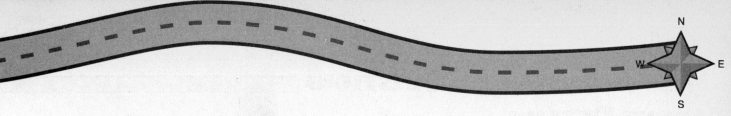

7. What is the *main* reason Lydia and Daniel are exploring the cave?

○ A to learn new things

○ B to become professional spelunkers

○ C to see stalactites

○ D to overcome their fear of the dark

8. What is the *main* reason Lydia's father is exploring the cave?

○ A to study the rock formations

○ B to make a map of the cave

○ C to show it to his daughter and her friend

○ D to test his miner's headlamp

9. Which of the following statements would the author of this piece be *most likely* to say?

○ A Caves are boring for explorers.

○ B Caves are spooky.

○ C Caves are often filled with surprises.

○ D Caves shouldn't be explored by children.

10. What is the *main* reason caverns are located in places with large deposits of limestone?

○ A Limestone is made from oceanic matter.

○ B Limestone caverns are more beautiful than other caverns.

○ C Limestone is filled with cracks and crevices.

○ D Limestone can be dissolved by water with traces of carbonic acid.

11. Which of the following elements is essential to the formation of caves?

○ A wind

○ B fire

○ C air

○ D water

12. What is the *main* purpose of the sixth paragraph?

○ A to paint a picture

○ B to provide information

○ C to create a mood

○ D to amuse the reader

Take your time !

MILE 6: ANSWERING QUESTIONS ABOUT DETAILS

Some questions will ask you about details from a passage. These questions can be easy to answer if you remember to do three things after you read the passage.

- Read the question and find out what you need to know to answer the question.

- Skim the passage looking for key words from the question.

- Reread the section of the passage where the answer is located.

Don't try to memorize all of the information from the passage. You don't need to, because you can always go back and read to find the answer.

Directions: Read each of the short passages below and answer the questions that follow. Underline the phrase or sentence in each passage that supports your response.

Eunice had a terrible thing happen to her when she reached camp. She couldn't open her suitcase! She forgot to ask her parents for the code to the suitcase lock before she left. Her suitcase contained everything she needed for the summer. She didn't know what to do!

Eunice tried calling home, but no one answered. She jumped on the suitcase, thinking it might pop open. But that didn't work. Just when she was about to cry, she remembered her mother had given her a card. She hoped the card would cheer her up. When she opened the card she saw that her mother had written, in large letters, "Don't forget the combination. It's 461."

1. Why did Eunice remember the card from her mother?

_____

_____

Rubber is one of the most important materials in the world. It's waterproof; it doesn't conduct electricity; it holds air and repels water; and it can block out or muffle noise. Without rubber, you couldn't ride a bike, wear sneakers, or water the lawn with a garden hose.

Europeans only discovered rubber when they began exploring Central and South America more than four hundred years ago. They found native Central and South Americans playing a game with a bouncing ball. Upon further investigation, they learned that the ball was made from a white liquid produced by a rubber tree.

2. Why is rubber so important?

_____

_____

As Dmitri strummed his guitar, he thought about his grandfather. His grandfather, Irving, had taught him to play the instrument. Irving had given Dmitri his first guitar when Dmitri was in second grade. Dmitri recalled sitting on his grandfather's front porch learning different chords. He studied his grandfather's long fingers while he played, and he listened to the notes.

"If you learn to play the guitar," his grandfather said, "you can spread joy wherever you go."

Dmitri often grew frustrated with his clumsy fingers. They couldn't seem to reach the right combinations of strings.

"Patience," his grandfather said. "Learning to spread joy with music takes time and practice. But you'll learn it's well worth the effort."

3. Why did Dmitri get frustrated when he was learning to play the guitar?

_____

_____

The word "quicksand" is enough to strike fear into the hearts of many people. In countless scary movies, characters have stepped into quicksand and then vanished, pulled into the ground by the mysterious substance.

Actually, there's nothing very mysterious about quicksand. Quicksand can be made of sand or soil that has water flowing up through it. That means you'll never find quicksand on a beach because the water is flowing down through the sand. Instead, valleys, bogs, riverbeds, and streambeds are the most likely places you'll encounter quicksand. That's because the sand or soil is floating on the water that is beneath it.

4. Where are the *most* likely places to find quicksand?

_____

_____

Landmarks help you find your way when you're on a journey. You might know you are going the right direction when you cross a certain river or see a certain building. The same is true when you're reading. You may see a word that you don't understand. However, the sentence in which the word appears and the sentences before and after it usually provide clues about the definition of the word. This is considered learning vocabulary in context.

Directions: Read the following passage. Use clues to figure out the meaning of the words in bold. After reading, look at page 37. Match the vocabulary words in column 1 with their definitions in column 2.

Twins

Ben and Naomi are brother and sister. They were born only four minutes apart. That makes them twins. However, they don't look anything alike. They also don't share any of the same interests.

Twins often look so much alike that you can't tell them apart. They may also share the same interests such as reading. Sometimes they'll have the same **mannerisms.** For example, if one twin moves her hands a certain way when she talks, the other twin probably does too.

There are two kinds of twins: fraternal and identical twins. Ben and Naomi are fraternal twins. This means that two separate sperm fertilized two separate eggs. This is rare because women's bodies usually only release one egg at a time. In fact, about one in ninety Caucasian women will have fraternal twins. Among other groups, the rate is higher. One in seventy-eight African American or Native American women have fraternal twins.

Even more rare are **identical** twins. Identical twins share the same physical characteristics such as gender, hair color, weight, and height. This occurs when a fertilized egg splits in two. As a result, identical twins have the same genetic

material—the chemical molecules that determine your physical traits. The causes of eggs splitting and creating identical twins are still a mystery. It happens about one time for every 250 births.

For years, people have debated why people act certain ways. Some argue that people are shaped primarily by **heredity,** the qualities inherited from their parents. Others believe that people are more influenced by **environmental** factors such as their surroundings, friends, community, and income.

Researchers used twins to explore this debate by finding identical twins who had been separated and raised by different sets of parents. Because the twins shared the same **genetic material** but had been raised in different homes, researchers hoped to explore how similar or different they were.

The results were surprising. Comparing **traits,** such as intelligence, behavior, and values, researchers found that the twins were very similar, even though they had grown up in separate places. This means that heredity influences human behavior in some very important categories.

COLUMN 1	COLUMN 2
mannerisms	inherited
identical	circumstances
genetic material	characteristics
heredity	exactly alike
environmental	habits
traits	chemical molecules

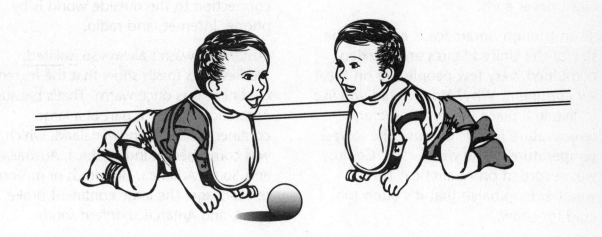

Name _____
Date _____

MAP CHECK 3

Directions: Read the following passage, and then answer the questions that begin on the next page.

Antarctica

The continent of Antarctica is located at the South Pole of our planet. Antarctica is a <u>continent of extremes</u>. Snow and ice cover the landmass, even though very little snow falls every year. For six months of the year, the sun shines twenty-four hours a day, but it's still very cold. That is because wind can blow up to 200 miles per hour, making it feel much colder than it actually is. During the other six months of the year, the night never ends.

Even though Antarctica is equal to the size of the United States and Mexico combined, very few people live on the icy continent. Why? How would you like to live in a place where the average temperature is ⁻49° Celsius? The lowest temperature in the world, ⁻89° Celsius, was recorded on Antarctica! The weather is so harsh that it's often too cold for snow.

While it doesn't snow often in Antarctica, there sure is a lot of ice. In some places, the ice that covers Antarctica is two miles thick. That's a lot of ice cubes! In fact, 70 percent of the world's fresh water is frozen in the continent. If Antarctica's ice were chopped and divided, every individual living on earth would receive a chunk as big as the Great Pyramid. Who could find a freezer big enough to store that?

Life is tranquil for the people who live on Antarctica. The continent has no history of war, and the frozen landmass belongs to everyone. That means you don't need a passport or a visa to visit. It's also a very solitary place to live. During the winter, Antarctica boasts a population of just twenty-eight people. To make matters more extreme, those twenty-eight can't leave the continent for more than six months. Their only connection to the outside world is by phone, Internet, and radio.

Antarctica wasn't always so <u>isolated.</u> Studies of its fossils show that the frozen continent was once warm. That's because Antarctica was once part of a large continent called <u>Gondwanaland</u>, which was comprised of India, Africa, Australia, and South America. Hundreds of millions of years ago, the large continent broke apart, and Antarctica drifted south.

In the midst of the frozen landscape, Antarctica has an active volcano, Mount Erebus. It is 12,447 feet high! The volcano has had an active lava lake for many years. This allows scientists to study the earth's mantle, which is a layer of earth located right below the crust.

Scientists also watch Antarctica carefully because of its effects on sea level. The ocean has risen about four to eight inches over the past hundred years. If

38

Roadmap to 5th Grade Reading: North Carolina Edition

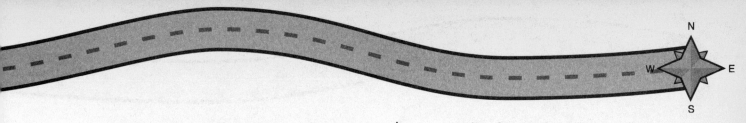

global warming continues, scientists believe that some of Antarctica's ice will melt. This will cause sea levels to rise approximately one meter over the next hundred years.

While this would be a significant increase, scientists are more concerned by what would happen if global warming caused large sections of ice that currently sit on land to break off. If this occurred, the pieces of ice would become giant icebergs that would displace great quantities of water in the ocean and cause sea levels to rise by as much as eighteen feet. Oceanside cities like Boston, New York City, and Miami would experience severe flooding.

It's difficult to predict whether this will happen. According to scientists, another possibility is that global warming would cause more snow to fall in Antarctica. This would cause a drop in sea levels as precipitation would be turned into ice.

One thing can be certain: Antarctica will continue to draw scientists and tourists to its arctic environment. Despite its harsh conditions, it is a fascinating continent.

Tip There's no need to memorize all of the information in a passage. After reading a question, skim the passage to find the part that you think will provide the answer to the question. Then read that part carefully.

1. Why does Antarctica receive so little snow?   *detail*

   ○ A It's too cold.

   ○ B It's too far south.

   ○ C It's too warm.

   ○ D It's always sunny.

2. Why is it believed that Antarctica was once part of a large continent called Gondwanaland?   *detail*

   ○ A There are accounts in history books.

   ○ B People remember when Antarctica and Africa were connected.

   ○ C The fossils found in Antarctica provide evidence that the climate was once warm.

   ○ D India and Antarctica share the same time zone.

3. Why do scientists predict that the sea level could rise by as much as eighteen feet?   *detail*

   ○ A They believe that Mount Erebus will erupt again.

   ○ B They think Alaskan icebergs are going to begin melting.

   ○ C They believe snowfall will increase as a result of global warming.

   ○ D They believe global warming could cause giant pieces of ice to slide off Antarctica.

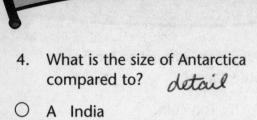

4. What is the size of Antarctica compared to?   *detail*

○ A India

○ B Mexico and the United States

○ C Africa and Australia

○ D South America

5. What do you think it means that Antarctica is defined as a "continent of extremes"?   *context clues*

○ A It is very hot and cold.

○ B It is a severe place.

○ C It snows a lot.

○ D It is a gentle place.

X 6. What information is **not** provided by the passage?   SKIP

○ A the types of plants and animals on Antarctica

○ B the thickness of the ice on Antarctica

○ C the number of people who spend winters on Antarctica

○ D the average temperature on Antarctica

7. Why is the weather still cold when the sun is shining twenty-four hours a day?

○ A Antarctica's elevation is high.   *detail*

○ B The ice makes everything cold.

○ C The wind blows extremely hard.

○ D The ocean temperature is cold.

X 8. After reading this article, you know that Antarctica is different from where you live in all of the following ways **except** for which one?   SKIP

○ A average income

○ B amount of ice

○ C population

○ D weather

9. What is the definition of the word *isolated* in the article?   *context clues*

○ A icy

○ B interesting

○ C difficult

○ D unreachable

10. How thick does the article say the ice can be on Antarctica? *detail*

○ A two feet

○ B fifty feet

○ C two miles

○ D two hundred miles

11. The Great Pyramid describes the size of what? *detail*

○ A the size of the house where people on Antarctica live for the winter

○ B the size of the entire Antarctic continent

○ C the size of the chunks of ice that everyone could receive from Antarctica

○ D the size of Mount Erebus, the active volcano on Antarctica

12. What does the word *tranquil* mean in this sentence? *context clues*

"Life is tranquil for the people who live on Antarctica."

○ A heartwarming

○ B dangerous

○ C difficult

○ D peaceful

13. What does it mean when the author says that Antarctica is a "solitary" place to live? *context clues*

○ A serious

○ B lonely

○ C diverse

○ D small

14. According to the passage, how much has the ocean risen in the last hundred years? *detail*

○ A eighteen feet

○ B two feet

○ C four to eight inches

○ D one meter

MILE 8: MAKING PREDICTIONS

Making a prediction means using clues to figure out what is going to happen. If you see dark clouds in the sky and hear thunder, your prediction could be that it will rain. You can also make predictions when you read. Clues in a selection can help you figure out what might happen next.

Directions: Read the following passage. Answer the questions as they pop up during the passage. Then read the rest of the story and see how close your predictions were.

The Boy Who Always Went First

1. Based on the title, what do you think the following story is going to be about? How do you think it will turn out?

    _____

    _____

    _____

    _____

THE STORY...

On the 75th floor of a very tall apartment building lived a boy named Ugali Zonta who led a charmed life. Everywhere Ugali went, and everything he did, he always insisted that he should go first. When he entered the elevator to whisk him up to his apartment, he cut in front of the other people waiting. You would think that someone might have shouted, "Young man, what on earth are you doing?" but no one did because Ugali had the most charming smile. His teeth were straight and white, and he had two nickel-sized dimples on each cheek. His eyes, the color of milk chocolate, sparkled when he smiled. In fact, Ugali's smile made people feel like they were being bathed in sunlight.

So Ugali went through life stepping to the front of lines, helping himself to the biggest pieces of cake, always getting the best ball or jump rope at recess. He would get the best seats at movies, and he never waited outside in the rain. As you can imagine, this made some of his classmates envious.

"I don't understand it," said Abel Aptner. "Both of my names begin with "A." It's not fair that Ugali, whose last name begins with "Z" should always go first."

"I agree," Cassius Coleman said. "Ugali thinks his smile is as good as gold, but I don't care that he has perfect teeth and has never worn braces. That doesn't mean he has the right to cut in line."

"Everyone thinks he's cute because of his dimples," Abel said. "I've got dimples." Abel poked his cheek with his finger. "If I press hard enough, I've got very cute dimples."

When Ugali's class played kickball at recess, the teacher chose two kids as captains, and the two captains, in turn, chose their teams. Ugali was a very good kickball player. In fact, he always kicked the ball so far into left field that he made home runs every time. So he was always chosen first for kickball games when he wasn't one of the captains.

Here was a situation that Cassius and Abel decided they could control. "The next time we're captains of the kickball teams," Abel said to Cassius, "neither of us will choose Ugali. Deal?" Abel stuck out his hand for Cassius to shake.

"Deal," Cassius answered, shaking Abel's hand.

2. What do you think is going to happen next in this story?

_____

_____

_____

3. How do you think the story is going to turn out?

_____

_____

_____

4. How have your predictions about the story changed since you began reading it?

_____

_____

_____

5. What has happened in the story to change your predictions?

_____

_____

_____

Mile 8: Making Predictions

THE CONCLUSION...

Of course, Cassius and Abel had to wait several weeks before their teacher, Ms. Wong, asked them both to be captains on the same day. When she called their names from her list and made them captains, they quickly glanced at each other, smiled, and nodded. Once in the hallway, the two boys gave each other high fives and ran outside for recess.

As usual, the whole class was gathered. And, as usual, Ugali was smiling his famous smile. Everyone was smiling back at him. Cassius and Abel flipped a coin to see who would choose first, and Abel won. He coughed, then cleared his throat. Before he uttered a word, Ugali began to walk toward him.

"Save your voice," Ugali said boastfully.

"I pick Dixon," Abel shouted.

Ugali froze in place. Dixon was the second best kickball player in the class.

"Well," Ugali said in a peevish way before he began walking toward Cassius.

Cassius bit his lip and pushed his hair off his forehead. "I choose Jackie."

Someone shouted, "Wacky Jackie?"

Jackie was the worst kickball player. Sometimes, he closed his eyes as the ball rolled closer, and he would miss it completely.

Ugali stood, opening and closing his fists, and his face turned beet red. Cassius and Abel could tell he was furious. They exchanged glances. What if a fight started? How humiliating would it be if Ugali beat up both of them? "Liz," Abel whispered. "Liz is on my team."

"Jeremiah," Cassius called out next.

As the two continued to call out names, the most astonishing thing happened. Ugali began to cry. With his face crumpled like a paper bag, he looked human again. Yes, he had dimples, his smile was friendly, and his eyes sparkled; but when he was crying he looked like an ordinary boy. Both Cassius and Abel felt so bad that they almost lost their resolve, and they almost said they had meant to choose Ugali first.

They didn't, however, and instead the strangest thing happened. Ugali stomped his foot and declared, "I'm sick of kickball. It's a stupid game. Who wants to play tetherball with me?" Smiling weakly, he looked at the other kids and then turned and marched toward the tetherball courts. Everyone was too shocked to move.

From that day on, Ugali played tetherball by himself every day. You could say that he was the first to discover the game of tetherball on the playground, and he's still waiting for the other kids to come and play with him. When they finally do, he will be the first in line, and the first to explain the rules to them.

6. Summarize what happens at the end of the story.

    _____

    _____

    _____

    _____

7. How does the actual ending compare to what you thought was going to happen?

    _____

    _____

    _____

    _____

MILE 9: DRAWING CONCLUSIONS

Great job! Now that you've practiced making predictions, you're ready to draw your own conclusions. Drawing a conclusion is similar to making a prediction. In Mile 8, you used information to figure out what would happen next in a selection. Now you will figure out something about a character or selection based on what you read. Look at the example below.

"Sally smelled the bottle of perfume and frowned."

Making a Prediction: Sally will not buy the perfume.

Drawing a Conclusion: Sally does not like the smell of the perfume.

Directions: Look at the picture below. Then write four conclusions based on what's happening in the picture.

1. _____

2. _____

3. _____

4. _____

Mile 9: Drawing Conclusions

Directions: Ten people are waiting in line to buy tickets to the county fair. The expressions, clothes, and possessions give clues about them. After studying each person, write one thing you can conclude about each person or pair in line.

1. _____

_____

2. _____

_____

3. _____

_____

4. _____

_____

5. _____

6. _____

7. _____

8. _____

Directions: Read the story below, paying close attention to the underlined sentences. Then answer the questions on the following page.

Tali didn't mean to upset the pig. After shoveling out the pen, she was hosing it down when she accidentally sprayed the pig with water. The pig squealed, then charged toward Tali, knocking her off her feet. <u>Tali screamed. She breathed in quick, short puffs of air.</u> The pig had knocked the wind out of her. She looked up. The pig was staring at her through its squinty pig eyes. It was strange. She'd always towered over the pig, and now it towered over her. <u>The pig's body was covered in sharp, bristly hair, and its nose was slobbery. Its hooves looked razor sharp.</u> Tali felt her heart begin to hammer in her chest. The pig had a strange look in its eye.

"Help," Tali screamed. "Someone help me!"

The pig sniffed. Tali's father had told her it was important to remain calm around animals because they could smell your feelings. She tried to take a deep breath. Was it possible that the pig could smell her fear?

The pig sat down with a heavy sigh right near Tali's head, and Tali almost choked. The smell of muck and slop was overpowering. What was she going to do? <u>If the pig rolled over, Tali's face would be pressed into its body. The thought made her stomach turn.</u> She needed help, but how could she call for help without arousing the pig's suspicion?

Just then, she had an idea. She would trick the pig by singing a song for help. She licked her chapped lips, swallowed, and then began to sing.

"I'm trapped in the pig pen

With a very angry swine.

If you come and help me

I'm sure I will be fine.

<u>The pig got angry</u>

<u>And pushed me to the floor.</u>

<u>Won't you please come and help me</u>

Escape through the door."

Tali sang the song sweetly and calmly, though her heart was pounding. Even though she was singing at the top of her lungs, the pig closed its eyes and began gently snoring. A thread of spit dribbled from its mouth.

Tali sat up quietly. No one had come to save her, but now was her chance to escape. <u>Holding her breath, she tiptoed from the pen.</u> When she was safely outside, she breathed a huge sigh of relief.

Living on a farm was always an adventure, but Tali hoped she never got stuck with the pig again.

1. Based on the sentences below, how does Tali feel?

   "Tali screamed. She breathed in quick, short puffs of air."

   _____

   _____

2. Based on the sentences below, how does Tali feel about the pig?

   "The pig's body was covered in sharp, bristly hair, and its nose was slobbery. Its hooves looked razor sharp."

   _____

   _____

3. Based on the sentences below, how will Tali feel if the pig rolls on her? What will she probably do?

   "If the pig rolled over, Tali's face would be pressed into its body. The thought made her stomach turn."

   _____

   _____

4. Based on the sentence below, why is Tali singing this song?

   "The pig got angry / And pushed me to the floor. / Won't you please come and help me / Escape through the door."

   _____

   _____

5. Based on the sentence below, why does Tali leave the pen this way?

   "Holding her breath, she tiptoed from the pen."

   _____

   _____

MILE 10: DRAWING CONCLUSIONS ABOUT AUTHORS' CHOICES

Take a deep breath. You've made it to the tenth mile! Guess what? It's very similar to the ninth mile. To draw conclusions about authors' choices, look for clues in the passage and ask yourself questions like, "Why did the author use this example?" and "Why did the author use this description."

Directions: Read the story b ~~p.39 pink Sh.Up.~~ **stions that follow.**

~~Author's Influence~~

Barnaby and Basil

An old man named Bar[nab]y [and his young daugh]ter, Basil, woke one morning and found the tongue of th[e ocean] [lapping] [their front] doorstep. By noon, the salt water had crept into the fr[ont] [hallway] [and] [stained] their Oriental rug.

Barnaby consulted his prized possession, an atlas, and then called his daughter to him. "Basil," he said, "the ocean is unhappy. It is time for us to pack our belongings and move to the forest."

Although her father had warned her that someday they would have to move, salty tears streamed down Basil's face. The ocean had been her constant companion. In the mornings, she strolled along the water's edge, looking for fancy shells and ribbons of seaweed to fashion into jewelry. In the afternoons, she sat in the small fort she'd built from driftwood. And in the evening, the ocean lulled her to sleep with its gentle sound.

Now, Basil looked out the smudged window of her father's house. She could tell the ocean was angry. It was metallic gray with dots of white foam. It pounded the sand, picking up and carrying away the driftwood. Her fort had disappeared, and Basil knew their house would soon follow. She took a deep breath. The salt still made her nose twitch, but now it also sent a shiver down her back.

Basil began gathering her most important possessions—her favorite shells and rocks, a quilt, binoculars, clothes, and books—while her father packed up the rest of the house. Then the pair set off for the forest. The path was long and steep, but they never looked back, even when they climbed to the top of the hill, a place that had once been their favorite place from which to survey the ocean. Both of their hearts would have broken to see the ocean behaving so violently.

After walking for many days, they finally reached the forest. Barnaby built a house from small logs while Basil carved furniture. At first, they were each so busy working on their house they didn't have time to think about leaving the ocean. But on the fifth night, Basil didn't fall asleep after sliding into bed. She lay there listening. The silence made her miss the lullaby of the ocean, and she couldn't sleep. In fact, she was up all night, and she watched the sun rise above the trees and wished they hadn't left their ocean home.

It was like this every night for a month. Dark moons grew under Basil's eyes, and she stopped speaking, except to say, "yes," or "no." Summer turned into fall, and one night as Basil lay in bed, her father came into her room.

"Listen carefully, Basil," he said. "The sound is there if you listen."

Basil cupped her hand around her ear and listened. At first, she heard nothing but her heart beating and air whistling in and out of her teeth. Then, she heard a whisper.

"It's the wind in the trees," her father explained. "It reminds me of the ocean in its gentle years."

And sure enough Basil could hear it—the wind flowing through the leaves and needle of the trees, like water flowing over sand. Her lips turned into a smile, and before she could say goodnight to her father, she had fallen fast asleep.

1. Explain how the author made the story enjoyable to read?

   _____

   _____

   _____

2. Why does the author include examples in the third paragraph of all the different activities that Basil does near the ocean?

   _____

   _____

   _____

3. The author writes, "dark moons grew under Basil's eyes." What does this line tell you about Basil?

   _____

   _____

4. What effect does the last line have on the story?

   _____

   _____

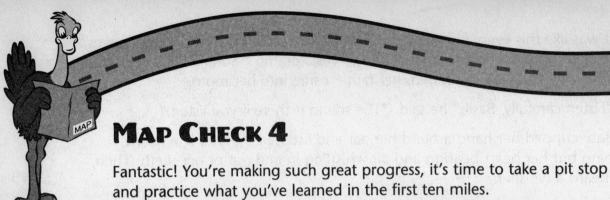

MAP CHECK 4

Fantastic! You're making such great progress, it's time to take a pit stop and practice what you've learned in the first ten miles.

Directions: Read the story below and answer the questions that follow.

On a Hike

We walked in a silent single file, like a snake. Fear kept us quiet. Overhead, thunder roared and distant lightning brightened the sky. We were above the tree line, exposed, and we knew we had to hike down quickly. Our boots were ankle deep in mud. Suddenly, the lightning split the sky in two. My hands tingled with electricity.

"Keep moving," one of our group leaders called.

There was more silence. If one person cried, we would all start crying. It was raining harder now. The drops felt like the tips of pins against my cheek. I shivered. My fingers were becoming numb.

"Jamie," I said, "do you think we're going to make it down?"

Jamie didn't answer. I turned to the person walking behind me.

"Beatrice, what's going to happen to us?" I asked. Beatrice was the oldest student in the group.

"Keep going," she answered. "And watch where you walk. It's slippery, but we need to get down fast."

This was hardly the answer I was expecting. I wanted someone to reassure me that we would get back safely. I stopped in the middle of the trail and crossed my arms.

"What do you think you're doing?" Beatrice hissed.

"I'm not taking another step," I answered. "Why did we come on this stupid hike in the first place?" I could feel tears welling up in my eyes.

Another wave of thunder rumbled, and a bolt of lightning cracked above us. Beatrice grabbed my arm and pushed me forward. "This isn't the time for talking," she said, "or for feeling scared. Just think about how each step is bringing you closer to taking a nice hot shower."

We sloshed down the mountain through a stream that hours earlier had been a dry trail. Several times, I almost gave up and sat down, but then I remembered what Beatrice said. I repeated, "hot shower, hot shower." Sometimes, I added, "chocolate bar, chocolate bar."

Finally, after what seemed like hours, we reached the trees. And then, all of a sudden, the storm ended. The sun burned through the clouds, and steam rose from the ground. It was strange how quickly things changed. Now it was hot! Instead of thinking about a hot shower, I began dreaming about taking a dip in the lake near where we were staying!

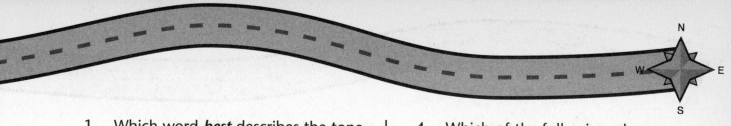

1. Which word *best* describes the tone set by the <u>first line</u> of the passage?

   ○ A tragic ✳
   ○ B laughable
   ○ C exciting
   ○ D ominous ✳

2. ✳How does the author show the severity of the storm?

   ○ A by revealing what the narrator thinks to keep herself going
   ○ B by describing how the storm makes the narrator feel
   ○ C by explaining how swiftly weather can change
   ○ D by ending on a humorous note

3. Why does the narrator dream of going for a swim at the end of the hike?

   ○ A Swimming in the lake was easier than taking a shower.
   ○ B Swimming was the only afternoon activity.
   ○ C The narrator began feeling hot.
   ○ D The narrator was very dirty and needed to get cleaned.

4. Which of the following phrases suggests the lightning struck close to the hikers?

   ○ A "My hands tingled with electricity"
   ○ B "thunder roared"
   ○ C "We sloshed down the mountain"
   ○ D "The drops felt like the tips of pins"

5. What do you think the narrator will probably do when she reaches the lodge?

   ○ A She will take a long, hot shower.
   ○ B She will call her parents and cry.
   ○ C She will read a book about lightning.
   ○ D She will start a water fight with Beatrice.

6. Why does the narrator stop and refuse to continue hiking?

   ○ A because of the lightning strike
   ○ B because her boots are muddy
   ○ C because she is scared
   ○ D because Beatrice grabbed her arm

✳ tragic = sad
✳ ominous = threatening
✳ severity = seriousness

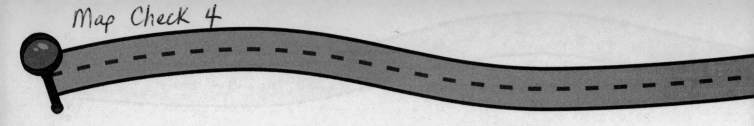

Directions: Read the story below and answer the questions that follow.

Treasure Maps

Treasure maps never fail to ignite the imagination. Left behind by pirates, prospectors, and explorers, these maps offer the promise of leading people to hidden treasures. Captain William Kidd, a famous eighteenth-century pirate, offered British officials his treasure map if they would agree to spare his life. They refused his offer, and since then, hundreds of people have searched, without luck, for Kidd's loot. Treasure hunters report that the treasure may be located in Canada, New York, or the Caribbean. It may not even exist at all.

Another famous treasure map was supposed to lead to a rich gold mine in Arizona. According to the tale, two German men saved a Mexican man from a saloon fight in the 1860s. To thank them, the Mexican man led the two to the gold mine. For years, Jacob Waltz, one of the two Germans, withdrew gold from it and killed anyone who ventured too close. As he was dying, he admitted to the murders and sketched a map, showing people how to reach the mine. Since then, many people have searched in vain for the hidden gold high in the Superstition Mountains near Phoenix. Does the mine really exist? It's a mystery.

As long as treasure maps exist, treasure hunters will roam the world, following ancient directions of suspicious origins. "There's no getting away from a treasure that once fastens upon your mind," said the author Joseph Conrad.

This is certainly true of the treasure left behind by a Scottish captain named William Thompson. In the mid–nineteenth century, he made off with tons of gold, jewels, and other valuables from Peru and hid them on Cocos Island, off the coast of Costa Rica. He never returned for the treasure. Before he died, however, he gave his treasure map to a good friend named John Keating. Keating reportedly brought home part of the treasure. Since then, hundreds of others have searched and returned empty-handed. There's speculation that a flood or rockslide changed the landscape of the island and made Thompson's map inaccurate.

Is Thomspon's treasure still hidden on the island? Perhaps, but we'll never be entirely sure. In 1978, Costa Rica officially banned all further treasure hunting on the island.

Before you begin reading a passage, you should always first read the title and introduction and predict what the passage will be about.

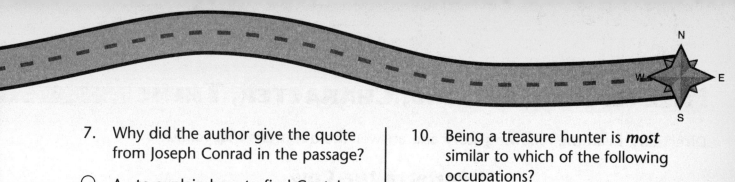

7. Why did the author give the quote from Joseph Conrad in the passage?

○ A to explain how to find Captain Kidd's treasure

○ B to describe a specific treasure to the reader

○ C to support the idea that people can become obsessed with treasure

○ D to make the passage less interesting

8. This passage is interesting to read because the author has included all of the following *except* for which one?

SKIP

○ A questions about whether treasures actually exist

○ B details about Thompson's treasure

○ C the story of the gold mine in Arizona

○ D instructions for creating a treasure hunt

9. In the third paragraph, what does the author mean when she says that treasure hunters will continue following directions of "suspicious origins"?

○ A Treasure maps are confusing to follow.

○ B Treasure maps can be very old.

○ C Treasure maps are wonderful mysteries.

○ D Treasure maps can be fake.

10. Being a treasure hunter is *most* similar to which of the following occupations?

○ A a gambler

○ B a lawyer

○ C a shopkeeper

○ D a doctor

11. Why does the article say that it's "a mystery" whether Jacob Waltz's mine exists in the Superstition Mountains?

○ A because Waltz was not very trustworthy

○ B because no one has successfully found it using Waltz's map

○ C because gold has not been mined from Superstition Mountain for decades

○ D because many people were killed trying to find Waltz's mine

12. If you were a pirate, what would be the *best* way to make sure that someone could find your treasure in the future?

○ A Leave the treasure on an island.

○ B Give a detailed map to a friend.

○ C Choose landmarks that wouldn't change over time.

○ D Hide the treasure in a cave or a cavern.

Directions: Read the following story and answer the questions that follow.

Henrietta the Cow

When Juan first set eyes on Henrietta, she was wobbling unsteadily and calling desperately for her mother. Then, Henrietta was no bigger than a dog. Now, she weighs over five hundred pounds.

Juan looked at her proudly. Tomorrow Henrietta would compete in the livestock competition at the county fair. Juan's eyes traveled around the barn on the fairgrounds, looking at the other animals. There were more than a dozen other cows, but none looked as beautiful as Henrietta. Her black and white spotted coat was shiny. Her brown eyes looked calm and happy. Her tail swished back and forth, beating a happy tune.

"You're going to be a star," Juan whispered in Henrietta's ear.

Juan had spent more than a year grooming Henrietta for competition. When she was a calf, he fed her milk from a bottle. Juan could still remember the first time Henrietta had licked his arm. Her bright pink tongue felt like sandpaper.

Juan took out a brush and began grooming Henrietta. Barns at the fair were always interesting. Next to the cows, there was a row of pigs. On the other side, there were hutches of funny looking rabbits with long, floppy ears. After cows, Juan's favorite animals were chickens. Juan liked animals like cows and chickens because you could keep them for pets, and they gave you food.

Henrietta was strong and obedient. Juan had taught her to follow him. When Juan pulled the rope left, she turned left. When he pulled the rope right, she turned right. It was sometimes difficult to persuade her to begin moving; Juan made a clicking sound with his tongue and cooed, "Let's go Henrietta, let's go."

Juan was hoping that Henrietta would be in a good mood tomorrow. "You're going to be very cooperative, aren't you?" Juan whispered. "You're not going to give me any trouble."

The judges would rate Henrietta based on her weight, general appearance, and training. Juan checked Henrietta's hooves to make sure they were clean.

"That's a pretty nice cow you've got," said a girl about the same age as Juan. She had braids in her hair, and she smiled at Henrietta.

"Thanks," Juan said. "Are you showing an animal?"

"No, I'm just here looking around," the girl answered. "My family lives in town, so we don't have room for animals. Did you raise her yourself?"

"Yep," Juan answered proudly. "I've been taking care of Henrietta since she was just six weeks old."

Henrietta heard her name and mooed. The girl laughed: "It sounds like you've trained her well."

Juan flushed with pride. Henrietta was a good cow. He ruffled the hair on her black nose. "She's a great cow," he answered. Suddenly, he was sure that Henrietta would do a terrific job in tomorrow's competition.

PLOT
What happened, and how did it happen?

_____
_____
_____
_____
_____

THEME
What is the theme?

_____
_____
_____
_____
_____

SETTING
Where did it happen?

_____
_____

When did it happen?

_____
_____
_____

CHARACTERS
Who was involved?

_____
_____
_____
_____
_____
_____

MILE 12: GETTING INSIDE A CHARACTER'S HEAD

Have you ever tried to see something from a friend's point of view? Perhaps you wanted to understand why your friend was angry, sad, or happy. You can do this with characters in stories, too. Read the passage carefully and pay attention to clues. As you read try to answer the following questions: How does the character look? How does he or she talk? How does he or she move? How does the character react to different situations?

Directions: Read the story and answer the questions that follow.

The Slippers

Once upon a time in ancient Egypt, there lived a wealthy merchant named Charaxos. One day, he was strolling through the market when he noticed a crowd gathering near the place where slaves were sold. He fought his way into the middle of the crowd where he saw the most beautiful girl in the world being set upon a stand to be sold.

Like Charaxos, she was Greek. Her skin was the color of marble, and her hair was as black as a raven. She was petite, with dainty hands and small feet no bigger than a doll's. Her beauty hypnotized Charaxos. Charaxos decided that moment that he would buy her. Because he was the wealthiest merchant in the area, he quickly accomplished his goal.

The walk home was awkward at first. Charaxos, after all, had just purchased her life, and the girl knew nothing about his character. "Tell me your name, my dear girl," Charaxos asked.

"I am Rhodopis," the girl answered in a voice more pure than spring water. "I was stolen from home by pirates and sold to a wealthy man who lived on the island of Samos."

Charaxos tightened his fists when he heard how she had been mistreated. "Go on," he gently urged.

"On the island, a small, ugly man named Aesop adopted me and treated me like I was his child. He tried to sweeten the bitter pill of captivity by telling me enchanting stories about animals and human beings. If it were not for his fables, I would not have survived my cruel fate."

Charaxos raised his eyebrows.

"When my rich master noticed how beautiful I had grown, he decided to sell me. That's how I ended up at today's market. I would weep, but I remember Aesop's stories about the importance of remaining strong." Rhodopis's eyes were glistening, but she bit her lip to keep tears from spilling from her eyes.

Charaxos felt his heart swell. What a brave and heroic girl! There was nothing he wouldn't do for her. In fact, he decided then that he would treat Rhodopis like a daughter.

As soon as they reached Charaxos's compound, he sent his servants scurrying to prepare a room for Rhodopis. Within a week, merchants of jewels and clothing had made many visits to the house, and carpenters had come, carrying lumber and slinging tools, and gone, leaving behind a house. The gardener hauled in loads of rose bushes, tulip bulbs, and strawberry plants, so that when Rhodopis stepped out the front door of her new house in her beautiful clothing she was greeted by the sweet scent of roses and strawberries.

When she smiled, Charaxos felt like his heart might melt.

One day as Charaxos was totaling his balance sheets, Rhodopis was swimming in the pool in her garden. The sun shone brightly overhead, and it was another hot summer day in Egypt. Only one solitary cloud swam lazily across the sky. Suddenly, however, Rhodopis noticed an eagle diving straight toward the pool. Rhodopis's servants shrieked and dove into the bushes, and Rhodopis froze in the pool. The eagle swooped down and plucked Rhodopis's rose-colored slipper from the edge of the pool, and then climbed back into the sky and vanished.

The sound of Rhodopis's weeping made Charaxos rise from his chair and run to the edge of the garden. "What is wrong?" he called out. "What is wrong?"

When Rhodopis told Charaxos about the eagle, he shook his head, wiped the tears from her cheeks, and sent a servant to buy new shoes immediately.

Life returned to normal. Rhodopis swam in the afternoons, and Charaxos attended to his business so that he could shower more gifts on his adopted daughter. Neither of them knew that the eagle had flown to the courtyard of the Pharaoh Amasis and dropped the slipper in the Pharaoh's lap. The ruler looked closely at the red slipper, admiring its excellent workmanship and tiny size. He felt sure that the woman who had lost it was lovely beyond belief.

The Pharaoh issued a decree, announcing that the woman whose foot fit the tiny shoe would become his bride, and he sent out his messengers to deliver it.

News of Rhodopis's beauty spread like fire through the kingdom. Messengers heard about the beautiful Greek girl living in the house of Charaxos and found the girl in her favorite place beside the pool. When they presented her with the shoe, she cried out. She had thought the shoe was lost forever. And when the messenger saw how easily it fit her foot, they wanted to take her to the Pharaoh immediately. The messenger also informed Rhodopis that the Pharaoh wanted to marry the woman whose foot fit the shoe. Rhodopis was overcome by the news of her good fortune.

Charaxos was saddened that his adopted daughter would leave the house. He paced back and forth in the garden. His stomach churned, and his heart seemed to be shriveling. When Rhodopis swept out of the house, looking more radiant than ever, Charaxos swallowed the lump in his throat and embraced her. Through happy tears, he whispered in her ear, "You are getting what you deserve, my dear. You are getting what you deserve."

Mile 12: Getting Inside A Character's Head

1. How does Charaxos feel when he first sees Rhodopis?

    _____

    _____

2. Write a sentence from the story that supports your answer.

    _____

    _____

3. After Charaxos hears the tale of Rhodopis's childhood, how does he feel?

    _____

    _____

    _____

4. Write a sentence from the story that supports your answer.

    _____

    _____

5. How does Charaxos feel when Rhodopis finds out that the Pharaoh wants to marry her?

    _____

    _____

6. Write a sentence from the story that supports your answer.

    _____

    _____

Directions: Choose three adjectives from the box that best describe Charaxos, the main character of the story. Write each adjective in the box at the top of each column below. In each column, list what Charaxos says or does in the story that tells you he could be described by this adjective.

Generous	Angry
Cold-hearted	Envious
Ambitious	Lazy
Sad	

Adjective #1

Adjective #2

Adjective #3

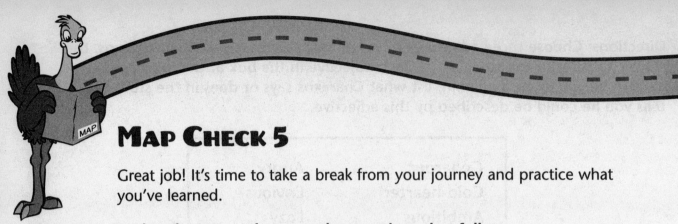

MAP CHECK 5

Great job! It's time to take a break from your journey and practice what you've learned.

Directions: Read each story and answer the questions that follow.

Birthday Soup

Everyone in the family wanted to do something special for Grandma Mabel's birthday. Aunt Louise, Uncle Jerry, Baby Didi, Helen, and Douglas gathered in the living room to discuss the birthday plans. "I think we should make a big pot of soup," Aunt Louise proposed. "Grandma Mabel loves soup, and we can eat it for dinner and tell stories."

Everyone agreed and went into the kitchen to begin cooking the soup. Aunt Louise was bending down to get the big soup pot from the cupboard when she bumped into Helen, who was dicing carrots. Helen dropped her knife, which just missed Uncle Jerry's toe. Jerry screamed so loudly that Douglas spilled the bag of potatoes that he was carrying.

Aunt Louise became red with frustration. "The kitchen isn't big enough for all of us," she screamed. "Everyone out, out, out!"

The family was used to Aunt Louise's outbursts. The only way to calm her was by leaving, and they slipped out of the kitchen. Aunt Louise wiped her hands on her apron and began to hum. She diced onions, chopped garlic, sliced carrots, chunked potatoes, and put the ingredients in a pot to cook. Then she went to the living room for a nap.

While Aunt Louise was snoozing, Uncle Jerry snuck into the kitchen. Aunt Louise was very bossy, and he wanted to defy her. Plus, Jerry wanted to add his own special ingredients to the soup. He lifted the lid and added four dashes of Tabasco, two pinches of sugar, and a whole lemon. Grandma Mabel was going to love the soup.

Baby Didi tiptoed down the hallway, looked cautiously left and right, and then scampered into the kitchen. Her favorite food was pickles, and she found a jar in the fridge. She dumped the whole jar into the soup pot.

Helen and Douglas had the same idea as the rest of the family. Because she loved dairy products, Helen added three dollops of sour cream and some grated cheddar cheese to the soup. Douglas loved spices and added a pinch of every spice in the spice cabinet. They both slipped back to their rooms to finish wrapping presents.

A potent smell woke Aunt Louise from her nap. At first, she imagined that Uncle Jerry had walked into the living room in his socks—his feet emitted a terrible odor! But after opening her eyes and sniffing the air, she realized the odor was coming from the kitchen. She sprung up from the couch and hurried to the kitchen. After lifting the lid from the pot, she screamed.

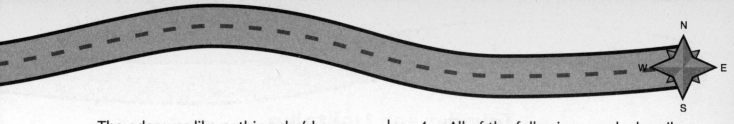

The odor was like nothing she'd ever smelled—worse than rotting leaves, worse than sour milk, even worse than Uncle Jerry's feet!

"What have I always said?" Aunt Louise demanded. "You should always let me do the cooking. I've said it a hundred times: Too many cooks spoil the soup."

1. Which character trait does not describe Aunt Louise?

○ A bossy

○ B angry

○ C frustrated

○ D sharing

2. Why does Baby Didi add pickles to the soup?

○ A because she wants to ruin the soup

○ B because she finds pickles delicious

○ C because she likes to anger Aunt Louise

○ D because pickles are the only food she likes

3. Which is the **best** description of Uncle Jerry?

○ A truthful

○ B hungry

○ C sneaky

○ D smelly

4. All of the following words describe Aunt Louise's state of mind after she wakes up from her nap **except** for which one?

○ A confused

○ B alarmed

○ C rested

○ D upset

Which word does not describe Aunt Louise after her nap?

5. Which character wants to rebel against Aunt Louise's bossiness in the kitchen?

○ A Uncle Jerry

○ B Baby Didi

○ C Grandma Mabel

○ D Helen

6. Which **best** explains why Helen and Douglas add new ingredients to the soup?

○ A They think that the soup tastes bland.

○ B They know that Grandma Mabel loves dairy products and spices.

○ C They are following a special recipe.

○ D They want the soup to include their favorite ingredients.

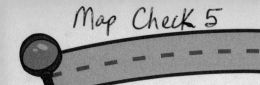

Thunder and Lightning

Once upon a time, there lived a young woman who had twin sons. Her husband was a cloud, and he lived far away in the sky. One day the boys went to their mother and asked, "Who is our father? We need to know our father so that he can teach us about the world."

Their mother stared into the distance. The sun was setting, and she pointed to the single cloud in the sky. "That is your father," she answered.

The boys' eyes opened wide in amazement. "Can we visit him?"

"Yes," their mother answered. "You may visit him, but you must make a difficult journey. First, you will pass by Wind, who is your father's oldest brother. He may try to blow you away and prevent you from visiting your father. You must be strong against him."

The beautiful young woman blinked away her tears when the boys set off on their journey. Her sons had never spent a night apart from her.

The boys traveled for many days across the plains and slowly climbed the great mountain in the east. Wind tried to blow them back, but they wrapped their arms around a tree, closed their eyes, and prayed for the storm to end. Wind exhaled another long breath of air. He loved to see people suffer. Finally, he got tired, and the boys continued on their way. The younger boy often stopped and looked into the distance. He doubted they would ever reach the clouds, but his older brother always pushed him forward.

The boys climbed higher up the mountain. At times, their vision was obscured by Mist, the younger cousin of Cloud. The older boy took his brother's hand and led him through the blanket of whiteness. Even though he sometimes trembled for fear of getting lost, he walked with great assurance.

"Are we almost there?" the younger brother cried.

His brother replied, "We'll know we've reached Father when it begins to rain."

In the morning, the sun was brightly shining, and the boys' hearts felt heavy. The sun drove their father into hiding, and the boys feared he would never reappear.

Finally, near the top of the mountain where nothing grew, they woke one morning and could see nothing. They were in the middle of a cloud.

"Cloud," called one of the boys. "Is that you, Father?"

"Yes," answered a voice. "I am Cloud, but who are you?"

"We are your sons," they cried.

"Prove it," Cloud said. "If you are my sons, then you can do what I do."

The older boy sent a streak of lightning across the sky and then the younger boy rumbled like thunder.

"Do it again," Cloud ordered.

The boys filled the sky with daggers of lightning and ear-splitting thunder, and the people living in the valley

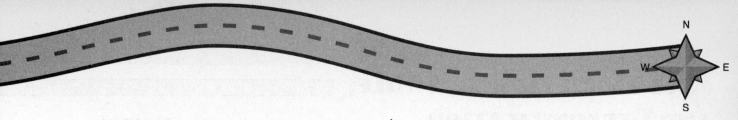

shuddered to see such a storm. Because Cloud has such a poor memory, whenever his sons visit him, they must prove they are his sons by producing both thunder and lightning.

7. How did the younger boy's attitude differ from his brother's on their journey to see their father?

○ A   He wanted to give up.

○ B   He was more excited to meet their father.

○ C   He was homesick.

○ D   He loved hiking.

8. Which word below **best** describes Cloud?

○ A   warm

○ B   vindictive = wanting revenge

○ C   outrageous = wild, incredible

○ D   forgetful

9. After the boys set off to find their father, which word **best** describes how their mother feels?

○ A   energetic

○ B   hopeful

○ C   sorrowful

○ D   enraged

10. Who served as the biggest obstacle on the boys' journey?

○ A   their mother

○ B   their father

○ C   Wind

○ D   Mist

11. Which words below **best** describe the older brother?

○ A   terrified and selfish

○ B   determined and brave

○ C   strong and intelligent

○ D   stubborn and foolish

12. Which of the following is the **best** description of Wind's actions?

○ A   deliberately protective

○ B   mean and pointless

○ C   unimpressive

○ D   kind and thoughtful

Tip

Use context clues to get inside a character's head. Context clues include things like how the character says things, how the character responds to different situations, and even how the character moves!

MILE 13: METAPHOR, SIMILE, AND PERSONIFICATION

To do well in your fifth-grade reading class (and the EOG Test in Reading), you should be able to identify and analyze figurative language. That includes being able to recognize a metaphor, a simile, and personification, which all make comparisons between two different things. These terms might sound complicated, but they're not. Once you know what they are, it's easy to understand how they're used.

I am a rock; I am an island: **Metaphor.**

After it rains, the pond is like an ocean: **Simile.**

The wind whispered in the darkness: **Personification.**

Directions: Write the terms listed in the box below next to the correct definitions.

```
Metaphor
Simile
Personification
```

1. a comparison between two different things that is formed with "like," "as," or "than"

    _____

2. a comparison between two things that is usually formed with a "to be" verb

    _____

3. a figure of speech that endows animals, ideas, or objects with human qualities and

    characteristics _____

Directions: Read the sentences below and decide what type of figurative language is being used in each sentence. Using the three terms from the box on the last page, write the correct type on the line next to each sentence. You may use the terms in the box more than once.

Simile, Metaphor, Personification

1. She turned as red as a beet after the teacher took the note she was writing and read it aloud to the whole class. _____

2. The cat jumped for joy when I finally returned from my vacation.

    _____

3. The moon is a spotlight, lighting up the woods around the cabin.

    _____

4. The tired, old truck gasped for air before chugging up the hill.

    _____

5. He snorted like a pig before stuffing more lemon meringue pie in his face.

    _____

6. Our house cried, "Don't leave," as we loaded the final box on the moving van and locked the front door for the last time. _____

7. Lollipop bushes and green coconut grass made the house look very inviting.

    _____

8. She was an elephant on the basketball court: slow and clumsy, but strong.

    _____

9. In the distance, the mountains looked like daggers. _____

10. The trees shook their fists at the gray, angry skies. _____

You've probably noticed how movies can change your mood. Some movies excite you, others make you laugh, and others make you cry. Stories, poems, and other reading selections also can make you feel things.

The mood describes the overall feeling of a passage. Determining mood is much like drawing conclusions. You use context clues, like figurative language, in the passage to help you. Pay attention to the way the scene is described and how characters speak and move.

Directions: Read the following passages. Then choose an adjective from the box below that best describes the mood of each and write it next to the passage. Circle the figure of speech and underline the figurative language in the passage.

Serious	Nonsensical
Humorous	Mysterious
Joyful	Sorrowful

The old woman cackled like a hen and shuffled down the stairs. The basement was pitch black and smelled like a swamp. "I'm coming," the woman cried.

The woman snapped on a light dangling from a wire. The basement was empty except for a giant box and next to it, a rocking chair. The woman knocked on the box. "Hello," she called, "Are you sleeping or are you awake?"

Mood: _____

Figure of Speech: Simile   Metaphor   Personification

Eliza Elizabeth was an elegant dandelion, a weed among women. No one liked her, and yet she attended all of the balls, dressed up in a yellow dress that was so bright that it nearly blinded everyone.

The other women tried to poison Eliza by whispering nasty things about her, but it never worked. Eliza would hear their cruel words, toss her yellow hair, and plant herself next to another dance partner.

Mood: _____

Figure of Speech: Simile   Metaphor   Personification

Matt knocked on the principal's door and then slowly entered. He stood up straight with his hands in his pockets, took a deep breath, and swallowed. "I have something to confess," he said. "I pulled the fire alarm."

The principal's face darkened suddenly like a storm sweeping across a sky. "Why on earth did you do that, young man?"

Mood: _____

Figure of Speech: Simile   Metaphor   Personification

"Today is upside-down day," Lucy cried, putting her boots on her ears and her wool cap on her feet. "Good night, Mother."

Her father looked confused. "It's morning still, and I'm your father."

Lucy began walking around the living room backwards. She told him, "Don't be as sharp as a butter knife." Out the window, the sun was shining. "Look out the window. You can't see anything because it's pitch black."

Mood: _____

Figure of Speech: Simile   Metaphor   Personification

The yellow lab looked around the playground, inspecting the other dogs, sniffed, then cast his sad eyes down toward the ground. His owner was nowhere to be found.

Just minutes before, he had been running around with a chocolate lab. His owner was standing next to the drinking fountain watching him. Then, he looked away and his owner disappeared. The yellow lab flopped down on the ground and began to whimper. He was hungry, and he wanted to go home.

Mood: _____

Figure of Speech: Simile   Metaphor   Personification

To analyze poetry, you need to become familiar with different elements of poetry. Once you've learned the definitions below, you'll use them to figure out the overall mood of a poem.

Directions: Write the terms from the box next to their definitions listed below. Then read the poem on the next page and answer the questions that follow it.

Mood	**Rhythm**
Theme	**Stanza**
Rhyme	

Words that end with the same sounds _____

The way the poem makes you feel _____

A grouping of two or more lines of poetry that are about the same length or share a

rhyme scheme _____

The musical beat of the words _____

The author's meaning or the underlying moral _____

Outside in the Weather

I'm going dancing in the pouring rain

I'll rock to the rhythm of the pitter-patter

If I get soaked, it doesn't matter

I'm going to groove until the rain goes away

I'm going strolling in the drifting snow

I'll march through the flurry of the tiny flakes

I may catch a chill, but who cares for goodness sake

I'm going to walk until the snow melts away

1.   How many stanzas are there in the poem? _____

2.   How many lines are in each stanza of the poem? _____

3.   Which lines rhyme in each stanza? _____

4.   Write an adjective that best describes the mood of the poem. _____

5.   Write one sentence that best describes the theme of "Outside in the Weather."

    _____

    _____

MAP CHECK 6

Directions: Read the poem below and answer the questions that follow.

Birthday

Now the cake

We must bake!

Blow up balloons

Dance to tunes.

Friends attend

And family too.

The room is filled

With happiness,

Happiness, happiness, to wish
you a happy birthday.

Birthday girl

With golden curls;

Grandpapa

Old and wrinkled;

Streamers flutter

Like your heart.

Shouts and cheers

For nine big years,

Happiness, happiness, to wish
you a happy birthday.

Burning torches

Light the porch;

Come and watch

Fireworks go off!

Let me light

Your fiery wand.

Let me place it

In your small hand.

Happiness, happiness, we wish
you a happy birthday.

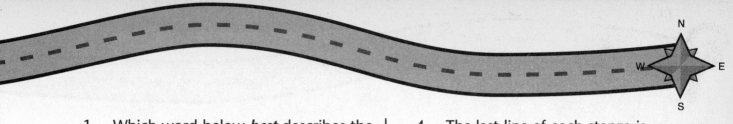

1. Which word below *best* describes the general mood of "Birthday"?

   ○ A   hilarious

   ○ B   critical

   ○ C   joyous

   ○ D   moody

2. From the poem "Birthday," what could the theme be?

   ○ A   Fireworks are an important part of birthdays.

   ○ B   Birthdays should be exciting.

   ○ C   Birthdays are happy occasions.

   ○ D   Friends and relatives make birthdays special.

3. Which lines rhyme in the first stanza of the poem?

   ○ A   the first and last lines

   ○ B   the first and second lines

   ○ C   the second and third lines

   ○ D   the sixth and seventh lines

4. The last line of each stanza is repeated for all of the reasons listed below *except* for which one?

   ○ A   to remind the reader to wish everyone a happy birthday

   ○ B   to unify the poem

   ○ C   to emphasize the joyfulness of birthdays

   ○ D   to make the poem sound musical

5. Comparing the heart to a fluttering streamer *best* demonstrates which of the following?

   ○ A   how scared the birthday girl is

   ○ B   how excited the birthday girl is

   ○ C   how fast the heart can beat

   ○ D   how impatient the birthday girl is

6. What is the birthday girl holding in her hand?

   ○ A   a piece of cake

   ○ B   a balloon

   ○ C   a flashlight

   ○ D   a sparkler

When you're reading poetry, read slowly and carefully. Make sure you understand each line before continuing to the next one.

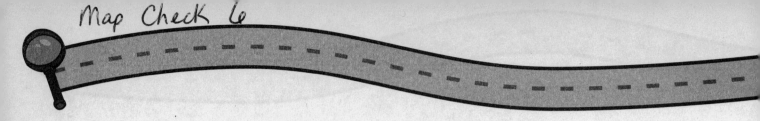

Map Check 6

Directions: Read the story below and answer the questions that follow.

How Zebra Got Its Stripes and Monkey Got Its Bare Behind

Long, long ago, when animals had just begun to roam the earth, it was always summer, and there was only a little bit of water stored in pools. As you can imagine, the animals greedily guarded their water. A loud, obnoxious monkey ruled one of the pools, proclaiming himself "Lord of the Water" and hoarding all of the water for himself.

Zebra and her son, Zizi, had just completed a long journey across the dusty plains. The sun had beat on them like a hammer, and their mouths were as dry as dead leaves. They were both having trouble swallowing when they sauntered to the monkey's pool.

The monkey was sitting next to a fire, roasting nuts for his supper. When he saw Zebra and Zizi, he bolted up and began waving his arms wildly. "Go away, water thieves," he hooted. "I am Lord of the Water, and I will not allow you to drink from my pool."

Zizi was outraged. Young and idealistic, he believed that all of the animals needed to live peacefully to survive the oven-like heat of the world. "This water belongs to everyone, not just you, ape-face," he said.

The monkey went bananas. He despised it when other animals confused him with the ape. It was insulting. They were two completely different creatures. "You have insulted me," the monkey screamed. "And you will never drink any of my water!"

Zizi and the monkey began to fight. Back and forth, and forth and back. Zizi tossed the monkey into the air, but the monkey did a somersault, landed on Zizi's back, and began pummeling him. Zizi bucked and threw the monkey on the ground and with a powerful kick, sent the monkey flying into the air. The monkey landed with a loud thud on a hard rock.

When he stood up, the fur on his seat snagged on a sharp corner of the rock, and he was left with a bare patch on his backside.

Zizi wasn't spared either. Having delivered such a swift kick, he stumbled backwards and landed in the monkey's fire. The flames licked his beautiful white coat, leaving black stripes of singed fur. Zizi bolted from the fire and galloped across the flat plains.

To this day, monkeys and zebras have kept their distance. Zebras avoid the rocky mountains where the monkeys make their home, and the monkeys still bark at everyone who trespasses.

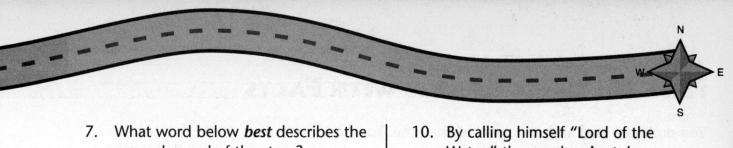

7. What word below *best* describes the general mood of the story?

○ A serious

○ B informative

○ C depressing

○ D light-hearted

8. What does the author want you to conclude from the story?

○ A Animals used to be able to talk.

○ B Zebras are stronger than monkeys.

○ C Being greedy never leads to good results.

○ D It is interesting how animals really got their characteristics.

9. Why is the sun compared to a hammer?

○ A because of the intensity of the heat

○ B because it plays a part in making things

○ C because it is hard

○ D because it shines like metal

10. By calling himself "Lord of the Water," the monkey *best* shows which of the following?

○ A how funny he is

○ B how respected he is

○ C how powerful he is

○ D how arrogant he is

11. When the author is describing the zebras' thirst, she compares their mouths to which of the following?

○ A sandpaper

○ B leaves

○ C ovens

○ D deserts

12. What did the monkey snag the fur of his backside on?

○ A an ice cube

○ B a nail

○ C a piece of firewood

○ D a rock

MILE 16: USING CHARTS WITH FACTS

You probably read and use charts all the time. You do it every time you look at a bus schedule to figure out when a bus is leaving or read the television guide to find out when your favorite program is on.

Directions: Below is a schedule of trains leaving from Washington, D.C., for cities around the country. Use the schedule to answer the questions.

Destination	Train Number	Departure Time	Arrival Time
Atlanta	789	8:00 A.M.	7:30 P.M.
Boston	345	11:00 A.M.	9:45 P.M.
Chicago	702	4:30 A.M.	6:30 P.M.
Denver	124	4:00 A.M.	8:00 P.M.
New Orleans	451	6:00 A.M.	4:10 P.M.
New York City	903	3:45 A.M.	9:15 A.M.

1.   What is the number of the train that leaves earliest in the morning? _____

2.   What is the destination of train number 702?_____

3.   What time does train number 789 leave for Atlanta? _____

4.   What time does train number 451 arrive in New Orleans? _____

5.   What is the destination city of the train that leaves latest in the day?

_____

Directions: Use the information from the box below to fill in the missing information on the chart that follows.

Cat's Meow trail takes 4 hours and is 6.5 miles long.	At the midway point is a one-room schoolhouse that was used in the nineteenth century.
The most difficult trail has a waterfall along the way.	Ann's Peak trail is 9.5 miles long.

Shark Tooth Mountain Recreation Area

There's a hike for everyone in the Shark Tooth Mountain Recreation Area. Use this chart to choose the perfect trail for you. It includes information on the length and difficulty of the hike as well as what you can hope to see along the way.

Trail	Length	Difficulty	Comments
Bollen Valley	3 Miles	◒	_____ _____ _____
Cat's Meow	_____	◒	This trail includes the best of Shark Tooth Mountain Recreation Area: great views, waterfalls, and hidden meadows.
Sunflower Meadow	1.2 Miles	○	There is a perfect place to picnic on this trail. The granite boulders make nice picnic tables.
_____	9.5 Miles	●	Great views of the whole valley. Be prepared to scramble up the last mile.
Three Streams	4 Miles	_____	On this trail, you'll see a beautiful waterfall at mile 2.

KEY
○ = Easy
◒ = Intermediate
● = Difficult

MILE 17: USING CHARTS WITH STORIES =- - - - - - -

Sometimes making a chart can help you figure out the connections between different ideas or characters in a story.

Directions: Read the following passage. Then use information from the passage to fill in the blank spaces in the chart on the following page.

Webster's Dictionary

Noah Webster was a wordy man. He studied law. He taught school. He wrote a spelling book. And he created *An American Dictionary of the English Language.*

Webster was born in the eighteenth century in the state of Connecticut. He attended law school until a family crisis brought him back home, where he taught school to support his family.

In those day, teachers didn't just teach. They did everything: They cleaned the school, repaired the roof, taught spelling, drilled arithmetic, and directed plays. Even though Webster wanted only to teach, he did all of the other chores cheerfully to set a good example for his students.

Eventually, Webster was able to tackle his first big project: writing the Blue-Backed Speller. During those times, words were spelled every which way, but Webster believed there should be a standard spelling for each word. That's why he wrote the book.

Because there weren't big companies to distribute books or giant bookstores where children could buy books, Webster rode his horse throughout the original thirteen states giving away free copies and taking orders from schools. The book was an enormous success, with more than a hundred million copies sold.

Webster was also ambitious. Not only did he want people to spell correctly, he wanted them to speak the same language. In those days Americans spoke English so differently from one place to another that they didn't understand each other. Webster thought everyone would live together more peacefully if they spoke one language, or "mother tongue."

For more than twenty years, he worked on *An American Dictionary of the English Language,* journeying around the country and overseas to learn the history of words and how they were first used. He changed the spellings of many words to ensure there were standard ways of writing them. For example, he changed "musick" to "music" and "plough" to "plow." Webster also standardized pronunciations so that everyone spoke the words in the same way.

At the end of his years of hard, solitary work, he published a dictionary of 70,000 words. Besides the Bible, it has sold more copies than any other book published in English. It's still around today. Although the Merriam family bought the rights to print the book, if you look around your classroom, you'll probably see at least one dictionary known as the "Merriam-Webster" dictionary.

Noah Webster created two well-known books. Write the name of the other missing book below. Then fill in the details about the books below the titles.

Noah Webster's Books

Blue-Backed Speller	1. _____ _____
Webster's first book 2. _____ 3. Sold _____ copies Webster delivered it on horseback	Webster spent more than twenty years writing it 4. _____ _____ Sold more copies than any English book after the Bible Contains 70,000 words

MAP CHECK 7

It's time to pull into a rest stop and check your oil pressure. The next two passages will give you a chance to practice what you've learned.

Directions: Read the weather forecast for five cities below. Then use that information to answer the questions on the next page.

City	Today's Weather	High and Low	Tomorrow's Forecast
Anchorage	61 degrees	high: 64 low: 52	Patchy morning low clouds. Becoming mostly cloudy with scattered showers by late afternoon. South winds increasing to 10 to 20 MPH in the afternoon. High low to mid-60s.
Chapel Hill	79 degrees	high: 88 low: 73	Hot and humid. Slight chance of showers and thunderstorms in the afternoon. High in the mid-90s. West wind 5 to 10 MPH. Chance of rain 20%.
Phoenix	97 degrees	high: 100 low: 81	Scattered showers and isolated thunderstorms. Cloudy and cooler. Chance of rain 50%. Highs from the upper 80s to mid-90s. Southeast wind 5 to 15 MPH, becoming southwest 5 to 15 MPH in the afternoon.
Raleigh	82 degrees	high: 88 low: 72	Hot and humid. Slight chance of showers and thunderstorms in the afternoon. High in the mid-90s. West wind 5 to 10 MPH. Chance of rain 20%.
San Francisco	64 degrees	high: 68 low: 54	Fog and low clouds in the morning. Clearing near the ocean and becoming mostly sunny inland by midday. Highs from around 60 coast side to the upper 70s in the warmest inland areas. Afternoon sea breeze 10 to 25 MPH.

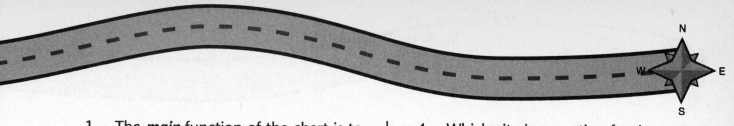

N
W E
S

1. The *main* function of the chart is to compare which of the following?

   ○ A amount of rainfall in different cities

   ○ B weather in different cities

   ○ C humidity in different cities

   ○ D number of sunny days in different cities

2. Which city recorded the highest temperature for the day?

   ○ A Phoenix

   ○ B Raleigh

   ○ C San Francisco

   ○ D Chapel Hill

3. In the chart, what do the symbols represent?

   ○ A the typical weather

   ○ B the high temperature

   ○ C the current weather

   ○ D tomorrow's forecast

4. Which city is expecting fog in the morning?

   ○ A Raleigh

   ○ B Anchorage

   ○ C Chapel Hill

   ○ D San Francisco

5. What is the weather *probably* like today in Durham, which is close to Chapel Hill?

   ○ A cool and breezy

   ○ B sunny

   ○ C thunderstorms

   ○ D clear and hot

6. In which city would you *most likely* want to wear a sweater?

   ○ A Chapel Hill

   ○ B San Francisco

   ○ C Raleigh

   ○ D Anchorage

Directions: Read the passage below and then answer the questions on the next page.

Fruit or Vegetable

Fruits and vegetables have been around for millions of years. But did you know that three hundred years ago, vegetables didn't exist? Well, actually, only the word "vegetable" wasn't around. Back then, any plant that was used for food was called a "fruit." That means in the seventeenth century nobody ever said, "Eat your vegetables, or you're not getting any dessert." Instead, people might have said, "Eat your fruit!" That could be any edible plant, ranging from lettuce to apples, from spinach to oranges, from cauliflower to pears.

In the eighteenth century, botanists—people who study plants—examined all of the plants that were called "fruit" and noticed important differences. They realized that some "fruit" came from the ovary of a flower and had seeds. They decided that these plants should be called "fruit." At the same time, the word "vegetable" was invented. "Vegetables" came to be known as plants that were eaten with meat or during a meal. To sum it up, "fruits" were plants with seeds, and "vegetables" were plants eaten during a meal.

Sounds logical, right? Nope. Some vegetables have seeds and are eaten during a meal. For example, cucumbers, eggplants, green peppers, tomatoes, and string beans all have seeds, and you've probably seen them at dinner. So which are they—fruits or vegetables?

Good question! In fact, it's a question that the United States Supreme Court had to answer approximately a hundred years ago. In New York City at the time, food importers—merchants who brought food from other countries to sell in the United States—had to pay special taxes to import vegetables, but not fruit. To avoid paying these taxes, one food importer tried to convince government officials that the tomato was technically a fruit and not a vegetable because it had seeds.

According to botanists' definitions, this was true. However, according to the Supreme Court it was not. They decided that tomatoes were vegetables because they were generally eaten during the main part of dinner and not for dessert. As a result, the food importer had to pay taxes on his shipment of tomatoes.

Today, that's how we generally decide whether something is a fruit or a vegetable. Fruits are usually sweet and eaten as a dessert or a snack. Vegetables, on the other hand, aren't very sweet, and we usually eat them during lunch or dinner with soup, meat, pasta, or other vegetables.

The next time your parents tell you to eat your vegetables—and you're having cucumbers, pumpkin, squash, beans, peas, eggplant, peppers, tomatoes, avocado, corn, or olives—you could tell them that they should technically be considered fruits. Then again, if you want dessert, you are probably better off just eating them. You don't want your parents to take you to court.

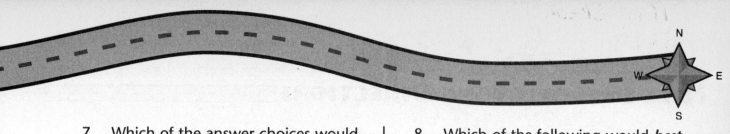

7. Which of the answer choices would **best** complete the graphic organizer below?

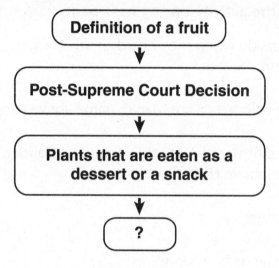

Definition of a fruit

↓

Post-Supreme Court Decision

↓

Plants that are eaten as a dessert or a snack

↓

?

○ A plants with seeds

○ B plants without seeds

○ C plants that are eaten during meals

○ D plants that are usually sweet

8. Which of the following would **best** complete the web below?

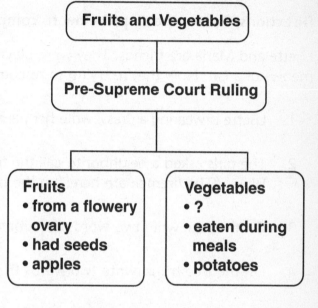

Fruits and Vegetables

Pre-Supreme Court Ruling

Fruits
• from a flowery ovary
• had seeds
• apples

Vegetables
• ?
• eaten during meals
• potatoes

○ A used for salad

○ B enjoyed with meat

○ C must be cooked

○ D hated by children

Mile 18: Following Directions

During almost every mile of this book, you've had to follow directions to complete the activities. The best strategy for following directions is to read them once quickly, then go back and read each step carefully.

Directions: Follow the steps below to complete the activity on the next page.

Lisette and Maria are friends. They were playing outside when they heard the desperate meows of a cat. Now they're trying to rescue it from the tree.

1. Lisette is wearing a dress; write her name beneath her. Write Maria's name above her.

2. The girls asked a neighbor to call the fire department before they found the ladder. Write, "The firemen are here!" in the bubble above Lisette's head.

3. On the sun, write two words describing the sun.

4. On the tree trunk, write two words that rhyme with "rough."

5. The squirrel wonders what the cat is doing in its tree. Draw an acorn in the squirrel's mouth. Above the squirrel, write three adjectives describing squirrels.

6. The dog chased the cat up the tree. Above the dog, write two things that dogs like to do.

7. In the leaves of the tree, write three words that begin with the fourth letter in the alphabet.

8. There are six steps on the ladder. Next to each step, write a word that begins with "L."

Mile 18: Following Directions

Directions: The instructions, utensils, and ingredients for making a cheese sandwich are listed below, but they are out of order. On the next page, write the ingredients and utensils needed for the recipe in the correct boxes on the top of the page. Then list the steps of the recipe in the right order in the box on the bottom of the page.

Cutting board

Bread

Spread mayonnaise on the bread.

Put the slices of cheese on the bread.

Mayonnaise

Take out two slices of bread.

Cheese

Cut cheese into thin slices.

Knife

Put the bread together into a sandwich.

Ingredients

1. _____
2. _____
3. _____

Utensils

1. _____
2. _____

Steps

1. _____
   _____
2. _____
   _____
3. _____
   _____
4. _____
   _____
5. _____
   _____

MILE 19: READING DIAGRAMS

To read a diagram, you must pay attention to pictures and descriptions.

Directions: Read the following passage and diagram.

There are nine planets in our solar system, each with unique features. Read the following passage to learn how they are similar to and different from Earth.

The Nine Planets

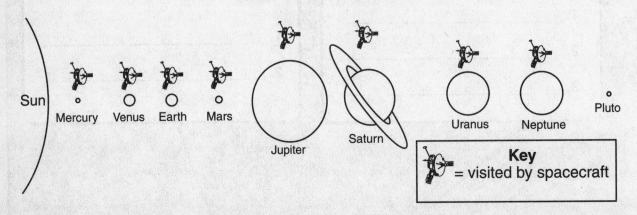

Mercury is a solid planet with extreme temperature changes. It can be as hot as 800°F and as cold as ⁻280°F. It has no rings or moons. (It is about one-third the size of Earth.)

Venus is a solid planet that is covered with clouds. Venus might have once had large water supplies, but they boiled away because of the planet's proximity to the sun. It has no rings or moons. (It is about the same size as Earth.)

Earth is a solid planet where water exists in a liquid state. In fact, 71% of Earth's surface is covered by water. This allows life to exist. Earth has one moon.

Mars is a solid planet with the tallest mountain—Olympus Mons at 78,000 feet tall—in the solar system. On average, temperatures on Mars are slightly cooler than those on Earth. Mars has two moons. (It is about half the size of Earth.)

Jupiter, the largest planet in the solar system, consists of gas. The enormous red spot on the planet is a hurricane. Jupiter has sixteen moons, as well as rings that can't be seen from Earth. (It is about eleven times bigger than Earth.)

Saturn is composed of gas. It has eighteen moons, the greatest number of any planet in the solar system, and seven rings. (It is about nine times bigger than Earth.)

Uranus is made up of gases, rocks, and ice. Twenty moons and eleven rings orbit the planet. (It is about four times bigger than Earth.)

Neptune has a small rocky core that is surrounded by gases. It has eight moons and four rings. (It is about four times bigger than Earth.)

Pluto is the smallest planet in the solar system. It consists of rock, with some water as ice. Because Pluto has an irregular orbit, sometimes it's closer to the sun than Neptune. It has just one moon. (It is about one-fifth the size of Earth.)

Directions: Use the words listed in the box below to fill in the blanks from #1 to #6.

Pictures	Parentheses
Labels	Written information
The title and introduction	Icons

1. Which part compares the size of different planets to Earth?

    _____

2. Which part shows the location of the planets with respect to the sun?

    _____

3. Which part tells how many moons each planet has? _____

4. Which part shows which planets have been visited by spacecraft?

    _____

5. Which part identifies the planets? _____

6. Which part explains the diagram's purpose? _____

Directions: List the appropriate planets below.

7. What is the name of the smallest planet in the solar system? _____

8. Which two planets are directly next to Earth? _____ and _____

9. Which planet is fifth from the sun? _____

10. Which planet is about the same size as Earth? _____

MAP CHECK 8

Directions: Read the following passage and answer the questions that follow to see how you're progressing on your journey.

Salt Garden

Is it possible to grow a salt garden? It sure is! The following science project will explain how to do it.

Project Materials

Porous rocks or pieces of coal

Salt (Regular salt dissolves easier.)

Cereal bowl (Use a larger bowl for a larger garden.)

Tablespoon

Warm water

Vinegar

Spoon

Fill the bowl about halfway with water.

Add a spoonful of salt to the water and stir until the salt has completely dissolved. Continue to add salt a spoonful at a time until it stops dissolving. At this point, the water has reached its saturation point. No more salt will dissolve in it. It should feel thicker and more difficult to stir than when you started.

Add a tablespoon of vinegar. The vinegar will help the water travel up through the rocks.

Arrange the rocks in your bowl. The rocks will be the foundation of your garden. You should make sure you like how they look.

Be patient. Although your salt garden will begin growing immediately, you'll have to wait a day or two before you notice any changes. Then you'll see salt crystals forming on top of the rocks. The salt crystals will grow more elaborate until all of the water has evaporated.

You might be wondering how this works. How does salty water turn into salt crystals? The salt water flows up through the coal or the rocks, depending on which you decided to use. It's important to use porous rocks because it makes the water's journey easier. The vinegar aids the process. Once the water reaches the surface of the rocks, it evaporates, leaving behind beautiful salt crystals.

You can practice following directions by cooking recipes or making crafts. Remember that the best way to approach directions is to read them through once completely and then follow each step carefully.

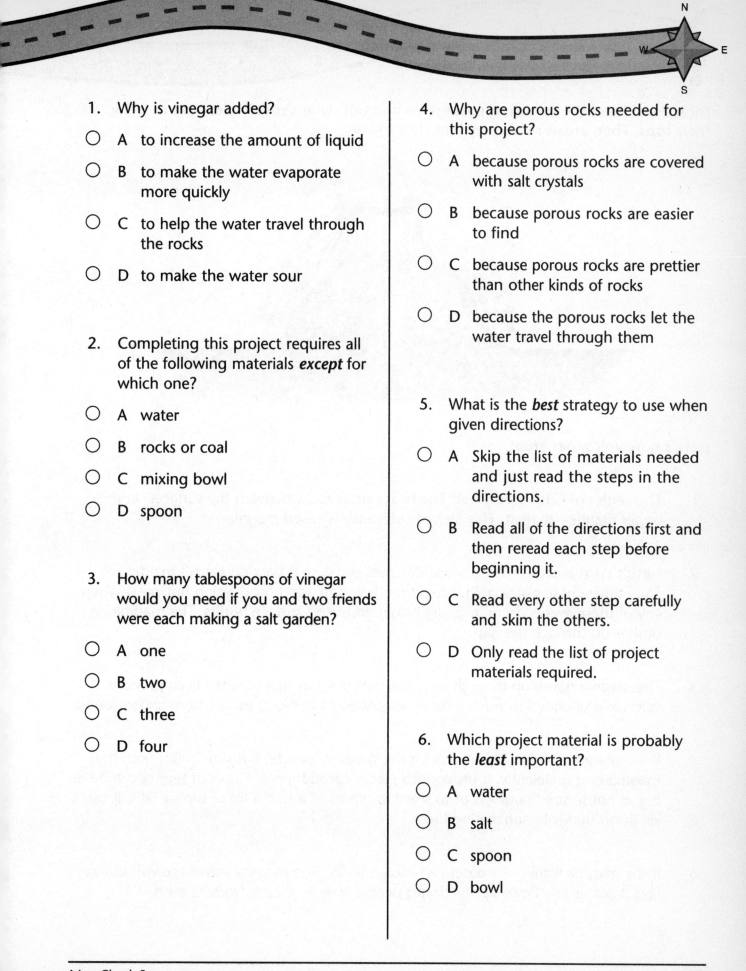

1. Why is vinegar added?

   ○ A to increase the amount of liquid

   ○ B to make the water evaporate more quickly

   ○ C to help the water travel through the rocks

   ○ D to make the water sour

2. Completing this project requires all of the following materials *except* for which one?

   ○ A water

   ○ B rocks or coal

   ○ C mixing bowl

   ○ D spoon

3. How many tablespoons of vinegar would you need if you and two friends were each making a salt garden?

   ○ A one

   ○ B two

   ○ C three

   ○ D four

4. Why are porous rocks needed for this project?

   ○ A because porous rocks are covered with salt crystals

   ○ B because porous rocks are easier to find

   ○ C because porous rocks are prettier than other kinds of rocks

   ○ D because the porous rocks let the water travel through them

5. What is the *best* strategy to use when given directions?

   ○ A Skip the list of materials needed and just read the steps in the directions.

   ○ B Read all of the directions first and then reread each step before beginning it.

   ○ C Read every other step carefully and skim the others.

   ○ D Only read the list of project materials required.

6. Which project material is probably the *least* important?

   ○ A water

   ○ B salt

   ○ C spoon

   ○ D bowl

Directions: Read the following passage to find out what causes volcanoes to blow their tops. Then answer the questions that follow.

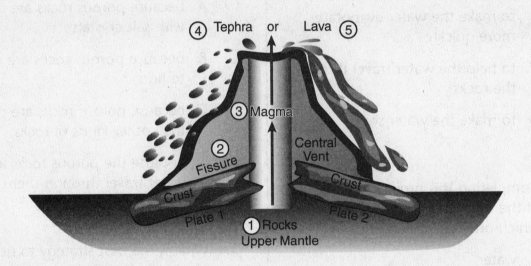

Here's how volcanoes erupt.

1. The center of Earth is very hot. The heat causes rocks beneath the surface—in the upper mantle—to melt. This melted substance is called <u>magma</u>.

2. Earth's crust is broken into sixteen different plates that float on Earth's mantle. Sometimes these plates get pushed together, drift apart, or develop hotspots. When any of these events occur, a <u>fissure</u> or gap in Earth's surface results. The magma pushes up through the gap.

3. The magma travels up through a <u>central vent</u> that has been created from previous volcanic eruptions. It is pushed up by violent gases trying to escape from underground.

4. If the magma is thick, it's difficult for the gases to escape. Pressure builds until the magma erupts violently. It breaks into pieces called tephra. Pieces of <u>tephra</u> can be as big as house-sized boulders or as small as pieces of ash. If a lot of tephra falls, it can kill living things by suffocating them.

5. If the magma is thin, the gases can escape easily. The magma leaves the volcano as <u>lava</u>. Lava usually flows slowly, giving people time to escape from its path.

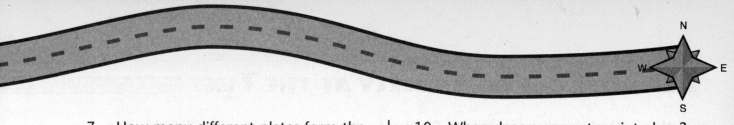

7. How many different plates form the crust of Earth?

○ A fourteen

○ B fifteen

○ C sixteen

○ D seventeen

8. Why did the author include a picture showing the inside of a volcano?

○ A to help you better understand and see what causes volcanoes to erupt

○ B to make the passage shorter to read

○ C to show different types of volcanic cones

○ D to show that magma can leave the volcano in the form of lava or tephra

9. Why did the author underline specific words in the numbered explanation?

○ A to draw connections to the picture

○ B to name the different stages of an eruption

○ C to show the spelling of unfamiliar words

○ D to focus attention on biological terms

10. When does magma turn into lava?

○ A when it's traveling through the central vent

○ B when it leaves the volcano

○ C before it leaves the surface of Earth

○ D after it pushes through a hole in Earth's crust

11. All of the following can cause a hole in Earth's surface *except* for which one?

○ A plates being pushed together

○ B plates drifting apart

○ C hotspots developing

○ D gases trying to escape

12. What is immediately above the upper mantle?

○ A Earth's crust

○ B the volcano

○ C the central vent

○ D lava

MILE 20: LOOKING CLOSELY AT THE TEXT

Directions: Read the passage below. On the next page, use the words listed in the box to decide which part of the passage fulfills each specific purpose.

The History of Money

In the Beginning was Bartering

Before money was invented, people *bartered.* This means that people traded goods or services they had for goods or services they wanted. Many individuals and organizations still exchange goods and resources, rather than using money.

9000–6000 B.C.: MOO!

Cattle and other animals (like sheep or goats) were the first type of money.

1200 B.C.: Find a Seashell, Pick it Up, and All the Day You'll Have Good Luck!

In China they began using cowrie shells as money, but people all over the world have used cowrie shells as money. Cowrie shells have been used longer and more widely than any other form of currency.**

1000 B.C.: Coin Necklaces

China was also the first place that people began using metal coins as a form of money. These coins were made of base metals* and often punched with holes so they could be strung together into chains.

640 B.C.: Precious Money

In Lydia (which is now part of Turkey), coins made of precious metals, such as silver, were created. The practice quickly spread to most of Europe.

A.D. 800–900: "You'll Pay through the Nose!"

In Ireland, tax evaders had their noses cut as punishment!

A.D. 806–1535: Potlach and Wampum

In North America, Native Americans used *potlachs* as money. Potlachs were ceremonies in which dances, feasts, and gifts were exchanged. North American Indians also used *wampum,* strings of clamshell beads, as money.

A.D. 1816–1930: The Rise of Gold

As more countries began using paper money, governments made banknotes worth a certain amount of gold so that the paper never became worthless.

**currency: money *base metals: metals, like lead and tin, that are not valuable.

Parentheses	Italics
Bold print	Title
Subheadings	Capital letters
Quotation marks	Asterisks

1. How does the author draw your attention to unfamiliar words?

   _____

2. What does the author use to introduce the main idea of the article?

   _____

3. What does the author use to define new words?

   _____

4. What does the author use to break the article into smaller sections?

   _____

5. Where does the author place examples of things?

   _____

   _____

6. What does the author use to note that something has been said?

   _____

7. What does the author use to emphasize different words?

   _____

8. What does the author use to make the titles seem different from the rest of the text?

   _____

You should be able to draw comparisons between two separate passages. To do this, first read each one separately, and then ask yourself what they have in common. A Venn diagram helps you to do this.

Directions: Read the poem and passage over the next two pages. When you're finished, answer the questions on page 98. Then complete the Venn diagram on the final page of the exercise.

One Night at the Pacific

Huge waves roll on to the beach,

Carrying a deadly lesson to teach.

The water breaks hard on the land,

Crashing beyond the world of sand.

The clouds are mean and scary in the skies,

Like looking at a monster in the gleam of its eyes.

The night was awful, people ran for cover,

Kids sought shelter while the storm did hover.

The rain, it seemed to last for ages,

Disturbing our homes and rattling our cages.

And when we thought the end we'd never see

The skies cleared, providing security.

Boating on a Sunny Day

When we set sail for the island in the Atlantic Ocean, the sky was as dark as the blue ink in Father's inkwell. It was perfect weather. The water was calm, and the wind blew steadily from the east, filling our sails nicely. The air was cool, but the sun was out, and soon, we were pulling off our sweaters and napping on the front deck of the boat. It was like this for several hours.

Father called out the warning. The wind died and then picked up, like someone blowing out birthday candles, a big strong puff. Flat, gray clouds came racing from the west, turning the sky from blue to gray to black. The sun fled. We began to shiver. The sea was frosted with angry whitecaps. Water slapped the side of our boat. It was angry, and our worthy boat rocked back and forth, creaking in pain.

We put on sweaters and raincoats. Father put on a wool hat. We put on boots. The wind howled. Before it could push us over, we pulled down the sails. A crow flew out of the darkness, landed on the boat, and began cawing, like a ringing bell, like a warning. Just then, the sea opened its mouth, and we plunged into its salivating jaws. The boat tipped right, then left. Then it spit us out roughly. The boat landed sideways, and water poured into the hull.

A strange expression—a mixture of fear and sadness—came over Father's face. He always told us that the sea was unpredictable, but we never believed him. Our sailing trips had always been calm. The ocean sucked us into its mouth again, and this time, we could feel its teeth crunching against the side of the boat. Now we understood why Father had always warned us.

Mile 21: Making Comparisons

1. What is the theme of "One Night at the Pacific"?

   _____

   _____

2. What is the theme of "Boating on a Sunny Day"?

   _____

   _____

3. How would you describe the mood of "One Night at the Pacific"?

   _____

   _____

4. How would you describe the mood of "Boating on a Sunny Day"?

   _____

   _____

5. Where is personification used in "One Night at the Pacific"? What does it represent in the poem?

   _____

   _____

6. Where is personification used in "Boating on a Sunny Day"? What does it represent in the story?

   _____

   _____

Mile 21: Making Comparisons

In the left side of the Venn diagram, list three characteristics of "One Night at the Pacific." In the right side of the Venn diagram, list three characteristics of "Boating on a Sunny Day." In the center of the Venn diagram, list three characteristics that are _shared_ by both "One Night at the Pacific" _and_ "Boating on a Sunny Day."

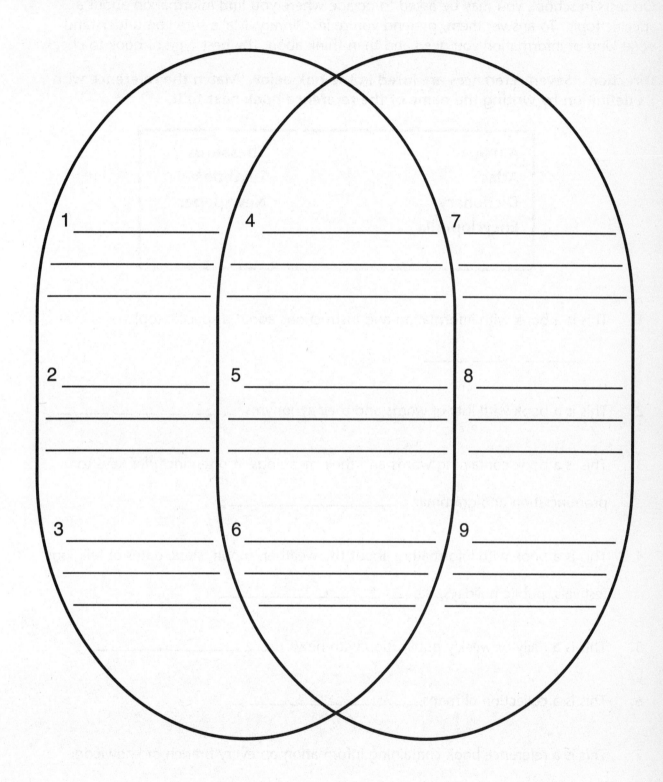

1 _____

2 _____

3 _____

4 _____

5 _____

6 _____

7 _____

8 _____

9 _____

On tests in school, you may be asked to decide where you find information about a specific topic. To answer them, pretend you're in a library. Make sure you understand what kind of information you need and then think about the best type of book to check.

Directions: Seven references are listed in the box below. Match the reference with its definition by writing the name of the reference book next to it.

Almanac	**Thesaurus**
Atlas	**Textbook**
Dictionary	**Newspaper**
Encyclopedia	

1. This is a book with information and instructions about a specific topic.

   _____

2. This is a book with lists of words and their synonyms. _____

3. This is a book containing words and their meanings. It often includes keys to

   pronunciation and grammar. _____

4. This is a book with information about the weather, moon, stars, dates of religious

   festivals, public holidays, etc. _____

5. This is a daily or weekly publication with news. _____

6. This is a collection of maps. _____

7. This is a reference book containing information on every branch of knowledge.

   _____

Directions: Read the questions below and fill in the blank spaces with the reference that you would use to answer each question. You may use the terms from the box on the previous page more than once.

8. What is another word for "amiable"? _____

9. Where is Libya located? _____

10. What is the definition of the word "catalyst"? _____

11. When is the next full moon? _____

12. How are black holes formed? _____

13. Who was Frederick Douglass? _____

14. How is the word "initiation" pronounced? _____

15. What's happening in the U.S. Congress this week? _____

16. What are the major events that happened in U.S. history before 1900?

    _____

17. What's the capital of Greece? _____

MAP CHECK 9

Congratulations! You've almost reached the end of your journey. Review what you've learned before you reach the finish line.

Do you ever forget things? Forgetfulness is a common experience. According to recent research, however, inventing things is also one of the mind's tricks. Not only does the mind forget things easily, it also has a tendency to make up things that never happened. This article explores the different tricks that the mind plays with memory.

Blocking

When is the last time you forgot someone's name? Or you remembered the first letter of a word, but couldn't remember the rest of the word? It turns out that people have greater difficulty remembering names than other words. That's because names are random. A woman whose name is Nancy doesn't necessarily look like a "Nancy." The brain stores the sound of the word in a different place than the meaning of the word. If there isn't a strong connection between the two, it's hard to recall the name of a person, even if you have met that person a dozen times before.

Misattribution

This occurs when the brain accidentally links two different things together such as a real event and an imagined one. After a tragic plane crash occurred in Amsterdam in the early 1990s, a group of Dutch psychologists* interviewed their colleagues to see how well they remembered television footage of the crash. Many had very clear pictures of the accident, when in fact, there had been no television footage. What the people "remembered" so clearly, they had created in their own minds from reading newspaper articles and talking to friends.

Suggestibility

Many people are guilty of this memory trick. It occurs when people confuse their own personal memories with other sources of information. "Leading questions or even encouraging feedback can result in 'memories' of events that never happened," psychologist Daniel Schacter told *Newsweek*.

A psychologist from Iowa State University proved this point with a simple study. He showed people a video of a man entering a store. Afterward, he told them that the man had murdered a guard. Then, he asked them to look at a series of pictures and identify the man they'd seen entering the store. Even though none of the pictures showed the actual suspect, the psychologist told a handful of witnesses that they had chosen the correct man. With this encouragement, many became even more confident that they had gotten a good look at the man who entered the store.

*A psychologist is someone who studies how humans think.

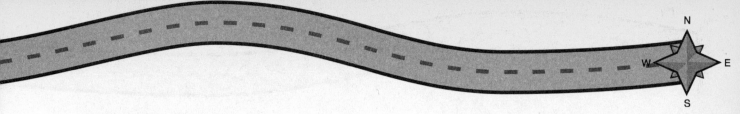

Persistence

People are more likely to remember terrible events than happy occasions. Although all memories are more powerful when they're attached to strong emotions, negative feelings cause the strongest memories. There's a physical reason for this. When you feel stressed out or very upset, your brain builds a stronger connection between the event and the memory.

Bias

It's a cliché, but it seems to be true. Couples who are in love usually recall only good things about when they first met; couples who are unhappy claim they could tell from the beginning that their relationship wasn't going to work out.

"We rewrite our memories of the past to fit our present views and needs," Schacter said.

Because people often can't quite remember their past feelings, they assume they are similar to what they're feeling in the present.

Tip

To answer questions about textual elements, go back and find the element to see how it's used. Textual elements such as subheadings, parentheses, and italics may be used differently in different passages.

1. Which would be the **best** place to get more information about memory and the mind?

○ A a dictionary

○ B a thesaurus

○ C an encyclopedia

○ D a history textbook

2. What would make this article easier to read and understand?

○ A quotes

○ B italicized writing

○ C footnotes

○ D a title

3. Why did the author of this passage use subheadings?

○ A to distinguish between different ideas

○ B to make the article longer

○ C to draw attention to important points

○ D to confuse the reader

4. How did you find out the meaning of the word "psychologist"?

   ○ A by reading it over and over again

   ○ B by reading the information in the parentheses

   ○ C by looking for context clues

   ○ D by reading the footnote

5. Why does the author include quotes from the psychologist, Daniel Schacter?

   ○ A to support different ideas

   ○ B to explain what leading questions are

   ○ C to make the passage more complicated

   ○ D to show how accurate memories are

6. How could you find more information about the plane crash in Amsterdam?

   ○ A by reading a textbook on flying

   ○ B by reading newspapers from the early 1990s

   ○ C by watching a television program about Europe

   ○ D by reading about Amsterdam in the encyclopedia

7. Which source would be *least likely* to help you find out more information about how memory works?

   ○ A a magazine interview with Daniel Schacter

   ○ B a book about different diseases that cause memory loss

   ○ C an encyclopedia article about the brain

   ○ D a diagram explaining how vision works

8. In the last section entitled "Bias," why is the sentence "We rewrite our memories of the past to fit our present views and needs" in quotation marks?

   ○ A It was spoken by Daniel Schacter.

   ○ B It provides the most complete explanation of why our memories are inaccurate.

   ○ C It proves that people who are in love don't tell the truth.

   ○ D It was printed in a newspaper.

9. Where would you find the *most* up-to-date information about recent discoveries on how memory works?

   ○ A an almanac

   ○ B an encyclopedia

   ○ C a thesaurus

   ○ D a magazine

10. When Daniel Schacter says, "Leading questions or even encouraging feedback can result in 'memories' of events that never happened," why does he use quotation marks around "memories"?

   ○ A to show that these memories are not true

   ○ B to prove we all have different memories

   ○ C to demonstrate how accurate all memories are

   ○ D to draw attention to the word

11. The author makes it easy to remember all of the different ways memories are not accurate by using all of the following *except* for which one?

   ○ A different sections for the different memory problems

   ○ B subheadings

   ○ C footnoted definitions of different memory problems

   ○ D text in bold print

12. When the author of the passage wants to introduce a new idea, what does she do?

   ○ A writes in the margin

   ○ B begins a new paragraph

   ○ C uses a footnote

   ○ D uses capital letters

13. Why is the word *Newsweek* in italics in this passage?

   ○ A because many readers may not know the magazine

   ○ B because it is not spelled correctly

   ○ C because it is the title of a magazine

   ○ D because the author wants to encourage everyone to read the magazine

14. What does the author do to help the reader remember different tricks the mind plays with memory?

   ○ A uses precise, scientific language

   ○ B defines the different tricks in parentheses

   ○ C puts the names of tricks in quotation marks

   ○ D divides them into different sections with subheadings

PRACTICE

TEST #1

INTRODUCTION TO PRACTICE TEST #1

You've finished all of the lessons in this book. That means that you've practiced all of the important reading skills for fifth grade. Way to go!

If you want to check your responses in the miles, all of the correct answers are on pages 168 to 184.

When you are ready, it's time to take the first practice test. The practice tests in this book are similar to the North Carolina EOG Reading Comprehension Test for fifth grade.

On the actual EOG Test in Reading, you will answer the questions on a separate sheet of paper. This sheet is called a "Bubble Sheet" because you have to "bubble" in your answers with a pencil.

The bubble sheet for the first practice test is on the next page. The bubble sheet for the second practice test is on page 139. That's right before the second test begins. You should tear out the bubble sheet or cut it out with a pair of scissors.

Try to take each practice test as if it were the actual test. That means you should follow all the test-taking rules and instructions. Fill in the bubble sheet and take the entire test at one time. Don't watch television or listen to music when you take the practice test.

Remember to use the tips and lessons you have learned and practiced in this book. They will help you to do your best. After you have taken the test, have an adult go over it. The answers and explanations to the practice tests begin on page 185. Find the areas where you need to practice more and review those lessons again.

Good luck!

PRACTICE TEST #1 ANSWER SHEET

Completely darken bubbles with a No. 2 pencil. If you make a mistake, be sure to erase mark completely. Erase all stray marks.

1. YOUR NAME: _____
(Print)　　　　　　Last　　　　　　　　First　　　　　　　M.I.

SIGNATURE: _____　DATE: _____ / _____ / _____

HOME ADDRESS: _____
(Print)　　　　　　　　　　　　　　　Number

_____
　　　　City　　　　　　　State　　　　　　Zip Code

PHONE NO.: _____
(Print)

2. YOUR NAME

First 4 letters of last name				FIRST INIT	MID INIT
A	A	A	A	A	A
B	B	B	B	B	B
C	C	C	C	C	C
D	D	D	D	D	D
E	E	E	E	E	E
F	F	F	F	F	F
G	G	G	G	G	G
H	H	H	H	H	H
I	I	I	I	I	I
J	J	J	J	J	J
K	K	K	K	K	K
L	L	L	L	L	L
M	M	M	M	M	M
N	N	N	N	N	N
O	O	O	O	O	O
P	P	P	P	P	P
Q	Q	Q	Q	Q	Q
R	R	R	R	R	R
S	S	S	S	S	S
T	T	T	T	T	T
U	U	U	U	U	U
V	V	V	V	V	V
W	W	W	W	W	W
X	X	X	X	X	X
Y	Y	Y	Y	Y	Y
Z	Z	Z	Z	Z	Z

3. DATE OF BIRTH

Month	Day	Year
JAN		
FEB		
MAR	0　0	0　0
APR	1　1	1　1
MAY	2　2	2　2
JUN	3　3	3　3
JUL	4　4	4　4
AUG	5　5	5　5
SEP	7　7	7　7
OCT	8　8	8　8
NOV	9　9	9　9
DEC		

© 2001 Princeton Review L.L.C.

4. SEX

○ MALE
○ FEMALE

The Princeton Review

Practice Test 1

1. Ⓐ Ⓑ Ⓒ Ⓓ
2. Ⓐ Ⓑ Ⓒ Ⓓ
3. Ⓐ Ⓑ Ⓒ Ⓓ
4. Ⓐ Ⓑ Ⓒ Ⓓ
5. Ⓐ Ⓑ Ⓒ Ⓓ
6. Ⓐ Ⓑ Ⓒ Ⓓ
7. Ⓐ Ⓑ Ⓒ Ⓓ
8. Ⓐ Ⓑ Ⓒ Ⓓ
9. Ⓐ Ⓑ Ⓒ Ⓓ
10. Ⓐ Ⓑ Ⓒ Ⓓ
11. Ⓐ Ⓑ Ⓒ Ⓓ
12. Ⓐ Ⓑ Ⓒ Ⓓ
13. Ⓐ Ⓑ Ⓒ Ⓓ

14. Ⓐ Ⓑ Ⓒ Ⓓ
15. Ⓐ Ⓑ Ⓒ Ⓓ
16. Ⓐ Ⓑ Ⓒ Ⓓ
17. Ⓐ Ⓑ Ⓒ Ⓓ
18. Ⓐ Ⓑ Ⓒ Ⓓ
19. Ⓐ Ⓑ Ⓒ Ⓓ
20. Ⓐ Ⓑ Ⓒ Ⓓ
21. Ⓐ Ⓑ Ⓒ Ⓓ
22. Ⓐ Ⓑ Ⓒ Ⓓ
23. Ⓐ Ⓑ Ⓒ Ⓓ
24. Ⓐ Ⓑ Ⓒ Ⓓ
25. Ⓐ Ⓑ Ⓒ Ⓓ
26. Ⓐ Ⓑ Ⓒ Ⓓ

27. Ⓐ Ⓑ Ⓒ Ⓓ
28. Ⓐ Ⓑ Ⓒ Ⓓ
29. Ⓐ Ⓑ Ⓒ Ⓓ
30. Ⓐ Ⓑ Ⓒ Ⓓ
31. Ⓐ Ⓑ Ⓒ Ⓓ
32. Ⓐ Ⓑ Ⓒ Ⓓ
33. Ⓐ Ⓑ Ⓒ Ⓓ
34. Ⓐ Ⓑ Ⓒ Ⓓ
35. Ⓐ Ⓑ Ⓒ Ⓓ
36. Ⓐ Ⓑ Ⓒ Ⓓ
37. Ⓐ Ⓑ Ⓒ Ⓓ
38. Ⓐ Ⓑ Ⓒ Ⓓ
39. Ⓐ Ⓑ Ⓒ Ⓓ

40. Ⓐ Ⓑ Ⓒ Ⓓ
41. Ⓐ Ⓑ Ⓒ Ⓓ
42. Ⓐ Ⓑ Ⓒ Ⓓ
43. Ⓐ Ⓑ Ⓒ Ⓓ
44. Ⓐ Ⓑ Ⓒ Ⓓ
45. Ⓐ Ⓑ Ⓒ Ⓓ
46. Ⓐ Ⓑ Ⓒ Ⓓ
47. Ⓐ Ⓑ Ⓒ Ⓓ
48. Ⓐ Ⓑ Ⓒ Ⓓ
49. Ⓐ Ⓑ Ⓒ Ⓓ
50. Ⓐ Ⓑ Ⓒ Ⓓ
51. Ⓐ Ⓑ Ⓒ Ⓓ
52. Ⓐ Ⓑ Ⓒ Ⓓ

53. Ⓐ Ⓑ Ⓒ Ⓓ
54. Ⓐ Ⓑ Ⓒ Ⓓ
55. Ⓐ Ⓑ Ⓒ Ⓓ
56. Ⓐ Ⓑ Ⓒ Ⓓ
57. Ⓐ Ⓑ Ⓒ Ⓓ
58. Ⓐ Ⓑ Ⓒ Ⓓ
59. Ⓐ Ⓑ Ⓒ Ⓓ
60. Ⓐ Ⓑ Ⓒ Ⓓ
61. Ⓐ Ⓑ Ⓒ Ⓓ
62. Ⓐ Ⓑ Ⓒ Ⓓ
63. Ⓐ Ⓑ Ⓒ Ⓓ
64. Ⓐ Ⓑ Ⓒ Ⓓ
65. Ⓐ Ⓑ Ⓒ Ⓓ

SAMPLE QUESTIONS

The Lion and the Elephant

The lion roared at the elephant resting in the middle of the river. "What are you doing in my kingdom?" he demanded. "You must have permission to be in my kingdom."

The elephant looked at him innocently and replied, "Why I'm just taking a shower." Then, he dipped his trunk in the water and sprayed his back.

Sample 1   Where is the elephant resting?

    A   in the city

    B   in the zoo

    C   in the jungle

    D   in the river

Sample 2   What kind of passage is this?

    A   a recipe

    B   a story

    C   an article

    D   a poem

Go to next page

Tankara and How the Lizard Lost His Tail

Every country has its own myths. This one is from Africa. It explains how lizards have come to lose their tails when they feel threatened.

Tankara the tortoise used up all of his salt, and his formerly delicious meals were now bland. To please his wife, he decided to pay a visit to his brother and ask him to spare some salt. Tankara's brother's salt stores were abundant, and he gladly shared his wealth. The only problem was that Tankara had no means of carrying the salt home. "I have an idea," his brother proposed. "I will wrap the salt in a piece of cloth and tie it up with a string. Then you can put the string over your shoulder and drag the parcel behind you."

"A brilliant idea," exclaimed Tankara, and he set off for home, dragging the salt behind him. Tankara's mouth watered as he imagined the tasty food he would cook, and he smiled as he pictured his pretty wife's beaming face. His brother was a generous turtle, and thinking this, Tankara hardly noticed the burning of the string across his shell. Suddenly, however, his parcel of salt snagged on something and practically pulled him off his feet. He turned around and saw a large lizard sitting on the parcel of salt.

"Get off my salt!" he cried. "This is a parcel of seasoning, not a city bus. If you need a ride, hire a horse."

The lizard gazed at Tankara lazily and said, "What are you screaming about? I was skittering along the path when I saw this mouth-watering bag of salt. Because I took possession of it, the salt is now my property."

"You are talking nonsense," Tankara said as quickly as a hare. "It is clear who owns this salt. I am holding the string that is attached to the cloth. That is proof enough that it is mine."

The lizard refused to budge, insisting that they visit the elders to have their disagreement settled in court. Tankara had no option and he reluctantly dragged his parcel of salt, with the lazy lizard sitting atop of it. They went to the court where a group of wise old men with long beards sat in judgment. First, Tankara detailed his case, speaking passionately about his challenges. Because of his tiny arms and legs, the only way he could carry his packages was by dragging them behind him. Then, the lizard took the stage, arguing "finders-keepers," an ancient law that stated that one could keep what one found.

The old men listened carefully. Many of them were friends of the lizard and knew if lizard received the salt, they would share in the spoils. Finally, they decided that the salt should be divided. Because the lizard found it in the middle of the road, he had a right to take half of it. The lizard leapt to his feet, flicked his tail, and took most of Tankara's salt. Poor Tankara was left to scrape up the little

Go to next page

Roadmap to 5th Grade Reading: North Carolina Edition

salt that had spilled on the ground. He left the court with a heavy heart.

Tankara's wife was not happy when she saw the miniscule amount of salt. It was hardly enough to season a casserole. She became more upset when she heard Tankara's sorry tale, and she demanded that he seek revenge. Although Tankara walked slowly, he was a swift thinker and he quickly devised a plan for payback. The next day, he headed for the lizard's house. When Tankara saw the lazy lizard eating a tasty meal of salted ants, he snuck behind him and grabbed him around his soft, tender belly. "Look what I found," Tankara called out loudly. "I was walking down the path when I found a lizard who belongs to no one."

The lizard was perplexed, but Tankara continued: "I think we should take this matter to the elders. Because they decided the salt case so fairly, let them decide this matter as well."

With great concern, the elders listened to both sides of the argument. They discussed it passionately in their chambers and returned to issue their ruling. "Because the bag of salt was cut in two," one elder said very gravely, "so too must the lizard be cut in two."

Tankara quickly seized a knife while the lizard begged for mercy. The lizard's pitiful excuses filled him with rage. At the last second, however, Tankara's heart softened, and he sliced off the lizard's tail, sparing his life. This is why lizards, to this day, lose their tails—from fear of losing their lives.

1. As Tankara left his brother's house, the following describes his state of mind *except* for which one?

   A   pained

   B   thankful

   C   bitter

   D   hungry

2. Why did Tankara take the lizard to the court the second time?

   A   He wanted to see if the elders would reach the same decision.

   B   He wished to argue his case in court again.

   C   He wanted to cut off the lizard's tail.

   D   He was trying to recover his share of the salt for his wife.

3. How did Tankara get revenge on the lizard?

   A   He asked his brother to trap the lizard.

   B   He stole salt from the lizard.

   C   He tied up the lizard with string and dragged him.

   D   He caught the lizard and claimed possession of him.

Go to next page

4. Why did Tankara have to drag the salt behind him?

A His arms and legs were too short to allow him to carry packages.

B The packet of salt was too heavy to carry.

C Carrying bundles on his back could cause his shell to crack.

D He wanted to please his wife.

5. This passage is interesting to read because the author does what?

A describes the court elders

B makes the conflict humorous at times

C explains why lizards and turtles aren't friendly

D tells why salt is important in cooking

6. After the court elders give Tankara permission to cut the lizard in half, which one of the following phrases *best* describes how he feels?

A greedy but triumphant

B tired but revengeful

C victorious but idealistic

D enraged but merciful

7. What does it mean that Tankara's brother's salt stores were "abundant"?

A They were delicious.

B They were hidden.

C They were sparse.

D They were plentiful.

Go to next page

Roadmap to 5th Grade Reading: North Carolina Edition

A Recipe for Good Writing

Do you ever have trouble deciding what to write? Preparing to write is like preparing for an athletic event. Often you have to warm up first in order to have a peak performance. The essay below will tell you what to do.

Do you ever sit in front of a blank piece of paper and panic? Have you ever crumpled up dozens of pieces of paper, frustrated by your inability to write something?

Published authors and beginning writers alike have faced writer's block at one time or another. Writing is hard work, and often the hardest part is simply getting started. If you don't allow yourself to get into the flow, you'll never know what you might be capable of creating. You might never discover your writer's voice or learn which subjects interest you.

Writing is a way of tapping into thoughts and ideas you weren't even aware of having. Once you begin writing, you'll be surprised by what you can learn about yourself. Writing regularly makes you feel less anxious about writing. You become better at expressing yourself using words. You get more in touch with your feelings.

"It's like running," says writing teacher Natalie Goldberg. "The more you write, the better you get at it. Some days you don't want to run and you resist every step, but you do it anyway. You just do it. And in the middle of the run, you love it. That's how writing is too."

Natalie Goldberg has taught writing workshops for the last twenty-five years. She believes that writing regularly is one of the keys to becoming a better writer.

Writing regularly can be difficult. Our minds can be nomadic. That means they like to wander. That's why it's important to focus. Here are some exercises you might try.

- **Making a List:** Keep a small notebook with you wherever you go. Whenever you hear or see something interesting, jot it down. Then the next time you write, look over your list. Choose a topic from the list and begin writing. Keeping a list of interesting things will help jumpstart the writing process.

1. *I saw an eagle chasing two seagulls. I wonder what was happening.*

2. *I heard a little girl say to her father, "Can we get a car without a top?"*

- **Writing Memories:** Memories are a rich source of writing topics. Something that happened to you can become the basis for a story, poem, or essay. Every few weeks, you may want to write down anything that you remember. It doesn't matter if it happened ten minutes or ten years ago.

I remember when I lost my first tooth. I wiggled and wiggled it, but I was afraid to wiggle it too hard because it would hurt. Then I was eating a piece of corn on the cob, and it popped right out.

Go to next page

8. Which of the following *best* expresses the main idea of this passage?

   A Writing well requires regular practice.

   B Writing well comes naturally to some people.

   C Writing should not be fun or creative.

   D Writing slowly can help you improve.

9. How do keeping lists and writing memories help with the writing process?

   A They teach writers punctuation rules.

   B They teach writers how to use dialogue.

   C They give writers instant subjects.

   D They make writers more anxious about writing.

10. The following are reasons for writing regularly *except* for which one?

   A You will understand yourself better.

   B You will discover your voice.

   C You will be able to write a best-selling novel.

   D You will have an easier time writing.

11. This selection answers all of the following questions *except* for which one?

   A What is the purpose of keeping a list?

   B When is the best time to write?

   C What does it mean when the author says "Our minds can be nomadic"?

   D How does practicing help you improve your writing?

12. What's the purpose of including the quote from Natalie Goldberg?

   A to define writer's block

   B to explain how to publish a book

   C to make the selection read faster

   D to give authority to the selection

13. For what purpose does the author include examples of how people completed the written exercises?

   A to show the kinds of things you could write

   B to help others think of their own memories

   C to share memories from her childhood

   D to prove that practice is important

Go to next page

Roadmap to 5th Grade Reading: North Carolina Edition

Creating Cascarones

Cascarones are confetti eggs that are an important decoration in some Hispanic festivals. Read this passage to learn how to make your own.

Project Materials

eggs

bowl

safety pin

water and towels

stuff to decorate the eggs

confetti material (e.g., tissue paper,

newspaper, writing paper, foil, wrapping paper)

scissors

white glue

small plastic funnel with dime-sized spout

First, decorate your eggs. Dip them into the dyes or color them with markers. If you're using a white crayon, write something or make a design on the egg. Then, dip it into the dye. The wax will repel the dye. The parts where you wrote will remain white.

While the eggs are drying, begin making the confetti to fill the shells. You can use a paper hole punch to make little circles of paper, or you can use scissors to cut paper into little bits.

Next, gently poke a pin into the bottom and top of a decorated egg. Make one hole bigger by rotating the pin, or poking the shell around the pinhole. Make one hole about the size of a dime. The bigger the hole, the easier it will be to remove the yolk and white from the egg.

Gently blow into the smaller hole. The idea is to blow the egg contents out the bigger hole. You may need to use the pin to break the yolk so that it will fit through the hole. Gently clean the empty shells.

Now, use the small funnel to fill the shells. After you've filled each one with as much confetti as possible, glue scraps of tissue paper over the holes.

Clean up your supplies and admire your eggs.

Finally, with your parents' and friends' permission, you can throw your eggs. When they hit something, such as a tree or wall, they'll explode in a burst of colorful confetti.

Go to next page

14. Which of the following materials are not used as confetti material?

   A   newspaper

   B   foil

   C   plastic wrap

   D   tissue paper

15. Which of the following items can be used to decorate eggs?

   A   balloons

   B   white crayon

   C   vinegar

   D   streamers

16. Why is a hole made in each end of the egg?

   A   to make confetti

   B   to make the egg easier to decorate

   C   to make the egg lighter to throw

   D   to allow the contents of the egg to be removed

17. What could be added to make the list of project materials more complete?

   A   how long the project takes

   B   suggested items with which to decorate eggs

   C   specific type of eggs to buy

   D   colors of paper to use for the confetti

18. What is the second step in making cascarones?

   A   making the confetti

   B   writing on the eggs

   C   blowing the contents out of the egg

   D   filling the eggs with confetti

19. For you to complete this project, what would be the best way to proceed after reading the instructions once?

   A   Change the order of the steps.

   B   Read the instructions backward.

   C   Gather the project materials.

   D   Read it over and over to memorize it.

Go to next page

The Kitten and Falling Leaves

by William Wordsworth

That way look, my Infant, lo!

What a pretty baby-show!

See the kitten on the wall,

Sporting with the leaves that fall,

Withered leaves—one—two—and
three—

From the lofty elder-tree!

Through the calm and frosty air

Of this morning bright and fair,

Eddying round and round they
sink

Softly, slowly: one might think,

From the motions that are made

Every little leaf conveyed

Sylph or Faery hither tending,—

To this lower world descending,

Each invisible and mute,

In his wavering parachute.

—But the Kitten, how she starts,

Crouches, stretches, paws, and
darts!

First at one, and then its fellow

Just as light and just as yellow;

There are many now—now one—

Now they stop and there are none.

Autumn

by Ralph Waldo Emerson

The leaves are falling, falling as
from way off

as though far gardens withered in
the skies;

they are falling with denying
gestures

And in the nights the heavy earth
is falling

from all the stars down into
loneliness.

We all are falling. This hand falls.

And look at other: it is in them all.

And yet there is one who holds
this falling

endlessly gently in his hands.

Go to next page

20. Which of the following statements **best** expresses the theme of "Autumn"?

 A   Every autumn brings fear because of the falling leaves.

 B   The stars fall from the sky periodically.

 C   Although everything falls, there is a force holding everything together.

 D   Autumn comes once a year.

21. In the first four lines of "The Kitten and Falling Leaves," which lines rhyme?

 A   the first and third

 B   the first and second, and the third and fourth

 C   the first and third, and the second and fourth

 D   the first and fourth, and the second and third

22. The mood of "The Kitten and Falling Leaves" is **best** described by which word below?

 A   somber

 B   funny

 C   playful

 D   thoughtful

23. What is the **best** approach to figure out the theme of a poem?

 A   Decide which lines rhyme.

 B   Ask yourself what meaning the poet is trying to convey.

 C   Try to figure out the literal meaning of the poem.

 D   Skip over all the figurative language in the poem.

Go to next page

Roadmap to 5th Grade Reading: North Carolina Edition

24. The words "falling" and "fall" are used repeatedly in "Autumn" for all of the reasons below *except* for which reason?

A to emphasize the end of everything

B to give the poem a serious tone

C to show how many leaves need to be raked

D to connect the different objects being described

25. What subject do both "The Kitten and Falling Leaves" and "Autumn" share?

A Both describe falling leaves.

B Both show kittens darting.

C Both describe the effect of the breeze.

D Both connect autumn to the other seasons.

26. In the fourth line of "The Kitten and Falling Leaves" the word "sporting" is used. What does it mean?

A conversing

B playing

C competing

D running around

27. How is the description of the autumn *different* in "The Kitten and Falling Leaves" and "Autumn"?

A The first poem is light, and the second one is darker.

B The first poem rhymes, and the second one doesn't.

C The first poem describes the decay of many things, and the second stays focused on the leaves.

D The second poem describes falling stars, and the first describes kittens playing.

Go to next page

Serena Williams

Serena Williams has wowed the tennis world. Read the following passage to learn more about this promising young tennis player.

Serena Williams is a tennis sensation. She's one of the first African Americans to break into the white-dominated sport of tennis. She has an older sister named Venus who's an equally talented tennis player. Both have spent most of the new century ranked in the top ten.

Born on September 26, 1981, Serena and her four sisters grew up in Los Angeles, California. Her father dreamed of all of his daughters becoming tennis stars, but only Serena and Venus showed talent. "Venus and Serena took to tennis as soon as rackets were put in their hands," said their older sister, Lyndrea.

The two sisters more than took to tennis; they shook the tennis world. At age four and a half, Serena entered her first tournament. According to her father, she won 46 of the 49 tournaments she played over the next five years. In the age-twelve-and-under rankings in southern California, she was ranked number one.

Serena's father made an unusual decision in 1995 and allowed her to begin playing professionally at age fourteen. In her first professional tournament in Canada, she quickly lost to an unknown. That wasn't enough to discourage her. Two years later, Serena was ranked 304th in the world and proved her worth by beating top player Monica Seles in a Chicago tournament.

Since then, Serena's ranking has improved steadily, and in September 1999, she won the U.S. Open. This made her the first African American woman to win a Grand Slam singles title since Althea Gibson in 1958.

Serena gave credit to her older sister, Venus, her biggest fan, toughest competitor, and most challenging training partner. "She was there supporting me," Serena said. "After I lost my first two match points . . . I saw Venus over there pumping me up." The next day, they both pumped each other up, and the dynamic tennis sisters triumphed in the U.S. Open doubles championship.

Go to next page

28. Which of the following is the *best* description of Serena's tennis career?

    A   expected

    B   remarkable

    C   unstable

    D   ordinary

29. What does the quote from Lyndrea, Serena's older sister, express in the passage?

    A   uncertainty about Serena's future

    B   surprise about Serena's U.S. Open title

    C   mystery about Serena's childhood

    D   evidence of Serena's natural ability

30. To find out more information about how Serena trains, which kind of Web site would be the *best* to visit?

    A   a Web site about top tennis stars

    B   a Web site on games

    C   a Web site on tennis equipment

    D   a Web site on getting in shape

31. How would you complete the graphic outline below?

Serena

U. S. Open

- wins Grand Slam singles title
- ?
- wins doubles tournament with sister

    A   turns professional

    B   practices eight hours every day

    C   joins Althea Gibson in making history

    D   beats Monica Seles in Chicago

32. Why does the passage call Serena a "tennis sensation"?

    A   She lost in a tournament in Canada.

    B   She and her sister play tennis together.

    C   She is a young and top-ranked American tennis player.

    D   She turned professional in 1995.

Go to next page

Autobiography from Mark Twain's *Roughing It*

The selection below is from a book that Mark Twain wrote describing a trip by stagecoach to the Nevada Territory in 1861. Twain and his brother, Orion, boarded the overland stage in St. Joseph, Missouri.

Our coach was a swinging and swaying cage of the most sumptuous description—an imposing cradle on wheels. It was drawn by six handsome horses, and by the side of the driver sat the "conductor," the legitimate captain of the craft; for it was his business to take charge and care of the mail, baggage, express matter, and passengers. We three were the only passengers on this trip. We sat on the back seat, inside. About all the rest of the coach was full of mailbags—for we had three days' delayed mail with us. Almost touching our knees, a perpendicular wall of mail matter rose up to the roof. There was a great pile of it strapped on top of the stage, and both the fore and hind boots were full. We had twenty-seven hundred pounds of it aboard, the driver said. . . . We changed horses every ten miles, all day long, and fairly flew over the hard, level road. We jumped out and stretched our legs every time the coach stopped, and so the night found us still vivacious and unfatigued.

* * *

In the evenings, the stagecoach stopped at way stations, places for travelers to rest and eat.

The station buildings were long, low huts made of sun-dried mud-colored bricks, laid up without mortar (*adobes*, the Spaniards call these bricks, and Americans shorten it to '*dobies*). The roofs, which had no slant to them worth speaking of, were thatched and then sodded or covered with a thick layer of earth, and from this sprang a pretty rank growth of weeds and grass. It was the first time that we had ever seen a man's front yard on top of his house. The building consisted of barns, stable-room for twelve or fifteen horses, and a hut for an eating room for passengers. This latter had bunks in it for the station-keeper and a hostler or two. You could rest your elbows on its eaves, and you had to bend in order to get in at the door. In place of a window there was a square hole about large enough for a man to crawl through, but this had no glass in it. There was no flooring, but the ground was packed hard. There was no stove, but the fireplace served all needful purposes. There were no shelves, no cupboards, no closets. In a corner stood an open sack of flour, and nestling against its base were a couple of black and venerable tin coffee-pots, a tin teapot, a little bag of salt, and a side of bacon.

* * *

Go to next page

Along the journey, Mark Twain and his party passed a wagon train of settlers going west.

Just beyond the breakfast-station, we overtook a Mormon emigrant train of thirty-three wagons; and tramping wearily along and driving their herd of loose cows were dozens of coarse-clad and sad-looking men, women, and children who had walked as they were walking now, day after day for eight lingering weeks, and in that time had compassed the distance our stage had come in *eight days and three hours*—798 miles! They were dusty and uncombed, hatless, bonnetless and ragged, and they did look so tired!

33. The information in this passage is easily understood because the author did all of the following *except* for what?

A   describe in detail different aspects of the journey

B   draw comparisons between traveling by stage and traveling in a wagon train

C   make a list of animals he observed along the way

D   use adjectives in his descriptions

34. Which of the following is not a change you can infer from the selection about how way stations or rest stops have changed since Twain's time?

A   construction

B   facilities

C   parking

D   selection of food

35. Why did Mark Twain travel west by stagecoach?

A   It was more comfortable than riding a horse.

B   It was faster than walking.

C   He liked traveling with the mail.

D   He was part of the wagon train of settlers.

Go to next page

36. The graphic organizer shown below is missing an item. Which is the *best* answer for completing it?

Traveling in the 19th century and present

Differences

- stagecoach
- ?
- way station
- walking
- covering distances slowly

- cars
- gasoline
- rest stops and restaurants
- driving
- traveling at 65 mph

A   conductor

B   horses

C   sod houses

D   hay

37. What is the *best* description of how Mark Twain felt when he was riding in the stagecoach?

A   excited

B   longing

C   free

D   crowded

38. To learn more about some aspect of stagecoaches, which of the following selections would be the *least* useful?

A   a story about a stagecoach conductor

B   a history of transportation

C   an account of western pioneers

D   a pamphlet published by the U.S. Postal Service

39. Which of the following expresses the *best* reason to read Mark Twain's story?

A   to learn more about traveling by stagecoach

B   to understand the life of pioneers

C   to learn how mail is delivered

D   to find out more about the construction of way stations

40. What evidence does this passage provide to suggest that it is an autobiography?

A   It describes a situation from a real person's perspective.

B   It provides lots of details.

C   It examines a historical event.

D   It is written with a sense of humor.

Go to next page

Matter

Matter is all around us. It makes up everything around us. Read the following passage to learn about the different states of matter and how matter changes from one state to another.

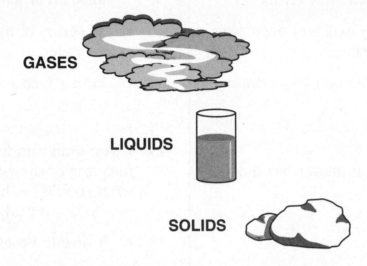

Here are the definitions of each state of matter and explanations of how matter changes states.

Solids: Solids are materials that hold their shapes. They do not need containers to give them shape. Solid matter becomes a liquid when heat or energy is applied to it. For example, heating an ice cube will turn it into water. (Ice, chairs, and your shoes are all examples of solids.)

Liquids: Liquids are materials that take the shape of the containers that hold them. Like solids, liquids are not easily compressed. That means if you have a cup of water it would be difficult to squeeze it into a half a cup of water. Freezing a liquid will make it a solid. Heating a liquid will transform it into a gas. (Water, soda, and wet paint are examples of liquids.)

Gases: The main characteristic of gases is that they will fill a container of any size or shape. Gases have the most energy of the three states of matter. Gases turn back into liquids when they are cooled. The energy gets subtracted from them if that happens. Heating a pan of water will produce gases. You know they are there because you can see steam rising from the water. (Steam, helium, and air are examples of gases.)

Go to next page

41. What is the function of the parentheses at the end of each definition of the states of matter?

A   to make the passage longer

B   to offer scientific terms

C   to further explain how matter changes states

D   to provide examples of the states of matter

42. Which state of matter has the *most* energy?

A   solids

B   gases

C   liquids

D   ice cubes

43. Which *best* explains why the author includes a picture under each state of matter?

A   to make the passage faster to read

B   to give an example from everyday life of each different state

C   to show different kinds of drinks

D   to show that the clouds and sky are both gases

44. If you wanted to find out more information on the three states of matter, what would you do?

A   buy a helium balloon

B   read an article about snow

C   experiment by boiling a pot of water

D   find a Web site on science

45. If you didn't understand the meaning of the word "compressed," what should be the first way for you to try to find out the meaning?

A   Consult a thesaurus.

B   Ask your parents what it means.

C   Look for clues in the passage where the word is used.

D   Try using the word in a sentence.

Go to next page

Beverly Cleary

Beverly Cleary is one of America's most beloved authors of children's books. Did you know, however, that when Cleary was young she hated reading? Read this passage to find out more about Cleary's life.

It is difficult to imagine that one of the country's most popular children's book authors was once a terrible reader. Born in McMinnville, Oregon, in 1916, Beverly Cleary moved to Portland, Oregon, in time to start first grade. Because she read so poorly, Beverly was assigned to the group lowest in her class. It was shocking because her mother was a school teacher. Her mother had also started a library before moving to Portland.

When it was reading time, Beverly felt her heart start to race. She squinted down at the words and tried to guess their meaning. She wanted to make her mother happy, but she didn't like reading. The sentences she read ("See kitty. See Mamma. I have a kitty.") put her to sleep. Instead of reading, she worried about how she would be punished for not reading.

It wasn't that Beverly's parents didn't encourage her to read. Looking back, she recalls that her mother read to her a lot. "We didn't have television in those days, and many people didn't even have radios. My mother would read aloud to my father and me in the evenings."

The school year ended. Beverly was allowed to continue to second grade, but only if she improved significantly. Luckily, second grade was an improvement. Her teacher was more patient, and Beverly slowly learned to read. However, this author-to-be still found reading boring and never picked up a book outside of school.

One dull Saturday when Beverly had nothing to do, she picked up the book *The Dutch Twins*. Actually, she just planned to look at the pictures. What a surprise! The story quickly captured her attention. She wanted to know what was going to happen in the story. She read all afternoon. After she had finished *The Dutch Twins*, she read another book by the same author.

Soon after, the library became her favorite hangout. She looked for books with stories that were similar to her life. Because she read so much, her teachers encouraged her. "When Beverly grows up," her seventh-grade teacher/librarian pronounced, "she should write children's books."

Beverly's mother was equally encouraging. She gave her this advice. "The best writing is simple writing," she said. "And try to write something funny. People enjoy reading anything that makes them laugh."

Beverly took her mother's words to heart, though she didn't begin writing immediately. After graduating from college, she worked as a children's librarian. Because she understood that reading could appear boring to children, she tried to help

Go to next page

them find books that would nourish a love for reading.

Encouraged by her husband, Beverly wrote her first book, *Henry Huggins* in 1950. One of the minor characters in *Henry Huggins* was a girl named Ramona. Ramona became one of her most popular characters.

Beverly says that she had no idea that Ramona would become such a popular character. "She was an accidental character," Beverly said in an interview. "It occurred to me that as I wrote, all of these children appeared to be only children, so I tossed in a little sister, and at the time, we had a neighbor named Ramona. I heard somebody call out, 'Ramona!' so I just named her Ramona."

Beverly eventually wrote many books about Ramona growing up. She wrote many other books as well. Since she began writing, she has published more than thirty books that have sold more than ten million copies. Many of her books have won awards, including the Laura Ingalls Wilder Award and the Newberry Medal.

Throughout her career, Beverly has tried to write books that she would have enjoyed reading as child. She says this is important. "I feel sometimes that [in children's books] there are more and more grim problems, but I don't know that I want to burden third- and fourth-graders with them. I feel it's important to get [children] to enjoy reading."

46. How does Beverly Cleary approach writing children's books?

A   Cleary thinks of subjects that will interest and give pleasure to children.

B   Cleary writes books that will sell well.

C   Cleary asks her husband for ideas.

D   Cleary spends a lot of time with children to find out their interests.

47. Which of the following expresses this passage's main theme?

A   Reading can be boring.

B   Try different hobbies until you find one that you like.

C   Parents need to read more to their children.

D   The way life turns out can be surprising.

48. Which words listed below *best* characterize Beverly Cleary's attitude toward reading when she was a child?

A   intrigued and nervous

B   frustrated and bored

C   gifted and anxious

D   calm and pleasing

Go to next page

49. This passage is fascinating to read because the author has written about all of the following *except* for which thing?

A a description of Beverly Cleary's writing process

B details about how much Beverly Cleary hated reading

C advice that Beverly Cleary's mother gave her

D information about Beverly Cleary's success

50. What made Beverly discover that she enjoyed reading?

A listening to her mother read fairy tales at night

B reading to younger children

C finding out that writers make a lot of money

D reading *The Dutch Twins*

51. What insight do you gain about Beverly when the passage says, "she tried to help [children] find the kind of books that would nourish a love for reading"?

A She thought all children should like the books she enjoyed.

B Finding a good book is difficult.

C Beverly was good at helping children pick out books.

D As an adult, Beverly remembered what it was like to be a child.

52. This passage would be useful for all of the following reasons *except* which one?

A to encourage children not to give up easily

B to teach children not be to be discouraged by things that give them difficulty

C to tell children how to write best-selling children's books

D to inspire children to read more

53. What is the author's attitude toward Beverly Cleary?

A bored

B intrigued

C furious

D disrespectful

Go to next page

Stonehenge

Read this article to learn more about Stonehenge, an ancient monument that has puzzled people for thousands of years.

About 137 kilometers southwest of London in Wiltshire, England, is a monument that has mystified people for thousands of years. Called Stonehenge, it consists of large stone slabs that are arranged and stacked in concentric circles. It was built more than 3,100 years ago during the Neolithic period. Stonehenge's sophisticated construction and long survival have mesmerized many people, leading viewers to puzzle over its original purpose.

Historians, astronomers, and archeologists have many competing theories about the purpose of Stonehenge. "Nobody really knows at all what [Stonehenge] was intended for," said Christopher Witcombe, an authority on the monument. "The fact that it was built over a long period of time makes it difficult to know if it maintained the same function over the time period or not."

One theory suggests that Stonehenge was used to mark the change in seasons. For most of the year, it's impossible to see the sunrise if you are standing in the monument's center. However, on June 21, the first day of summer, you can see the rising sun from the center. In fact, it appears to balance on one of the main stones. The same thing occurs on the first day of winter, except it's the sunset on the opposite side that's visible.

But what does this mean? Some have argued that farmers used Stonehenge to keep track of the changing seasons. Others believe that Stonehenge was used as a religious temple. Burial mounds surround the monument, suggesting that Stonehenge held spiritual significance for people.

Yet another theory is that Stonehenge was used for astronomical purposes. People believe that the stones could predict eclipses. The astronomer Fred Hoyle has made the strongest case for this theory. "I set myself the clear-cut target of finding out if the stones that exist at Stonehenge could, in fact, be used to predict eclipses—and it seemed to me they could."

While there are many theories, there are still no easy answers to unlock the mystery of Stonehenge. Witcombe believes that it's important to be open-minded. "In some cases, some of these ideas may initially sound a bit wacky, but you never know—there may be one or two aspects of them which may indeed have some bearing."

Go to next page

54. What is the *best* strategy to follow before you begin reading a passage?

  A   Ask your teacher what the passage is about.

  B   Determine how many more passages you have to read and budget your time.

  C   Count how many words there are in the passage.

  D   Predict the subject of the passage by reading the title and introduction.

55. In the final paragraph, why are there quotation marks around the last sentence?

  A   They are the words of Fred Hoyle.

  B   It is the most important part of the passage.

  C   It proves that Stonehenge is a mystery.

  D   It is a comment made by the Stonehenge expert Christopher Witcombe.

56. Which source below would have the *most* up-to-date information about Stonehenge?

  A   a travel book about Europe

  B   a current magazine devoted to architectural mysteries

  C   an encyclopedia

  D   a modern dictionary

57. Which evidence suggests that Stonehenge was a religious temple?

  A   seeing the rising sun from the center of the monument

  B   the concentric circles

  C   burial mounds surrounding the monument

  D   Stonehenge's sophisticated construction

58. Which phrase from the passage supports the idea that Stonehenge arouses curiosity?

  A   "Burial mounds surround the monument"

  B   "the stones could be used to predict eclipses"

  C   "leading viewers to puzzle over its original purpose"

  D   "there are still no easy answers"

59. The "Stonehenge" passage would offer the *most* helpful information for undertaking which of the following research papers?

  A   architectural mysteries

  B   history of architecture

  C   European monuments

  D   astronomy in England

Go to next page

The Combination

Read the story below about a forgetful father and his clever family.

Father left a combination lock and a note on the dining room table. He left them there before departing on a week-long fishing trip from our island home.

According to the note, my father had programmed the lock but promptly forgotten the combination. He thought he'd set the combination to a number that would be easy to remember, but he had somehow forgotten it.

The combination could be his birthday, or the year he was born. Or it could be my mother's birthday, or it could be the year of one of our birthdays. He was offering a $20 reward to the person who could crack the combination. Always eager to make some money, my brother, Scott, grabbed the lock first.

He fiddled with the lock for over an hour. "What was the year Father was born?" Scott asked my mother and me as we cooked dinner.

"1942," my mother answered.

But that didn't work. Soon, after Scott tried every possible combination of our birthdays, he threw the lock down in disgust.

The next day, I put the lock in my pocket and carried it down to the marina to try to earn Father's $20 reward as I watched the boats come sailing in. I flicked some numbers into place, and then yanked the lock, hoping it would open. But it didn't budge. Once the wind came up and foam started frosting the sea, I gave up and went home.

That evening, my mother sat out on the deck, taking her turn at trying to crack the mystery. Her brow was knit in concentration as she spun the lock's numbers. She worked until the sun slipped behind a nearby island.

"Let's put our heads together," my mother announced to us, "and see whether we can think the way Father thinks."

The three of us gathered back on the deck, trying to think like our forgetful father. Overhead, seagulls squawked.

Mother spoke first. "He has a terrible habit of reversing numbers. Instead of writing 19, he sometimes writes 91."

"And sometimes he gets confused and thinks I was born in 1974, instead of 1984," my brother said.

"I have an idea," I said. "What if he mixed up the year of Scott's birthday, reversed it, and programmed in 4791?"

Mother spun the numbers into place, while my brother and I waited to see what would happen. Sure enough, the lock opened! And because the three of us had solved the puzzle together, we split the money into thirds, went directly to the store, and bought food for a picnic.

Go to next page

60. Why do you suppose the author wrote this story?

   A   to describe life on an island

   B   to tell about a family tragedy

   C   to show how a problem is solved

   D   to provide a description of a normal family

61. Why is the family able to figure out the forgotten combination?

   A   Scott is good at figuring out puzzles.

   B   Scott is the only one who knows everyone's birthday.

   C   They worked alone.

   D   They know the kind of mistakes that Father is likely to make.

62. In what year was the forgetful father born?

   A   1942

   B   1974

   C   1984

   D   1990

63. What is the *best* moral of this story from the choices listed below?

   A   Working alone is the best way to solve a problem.

   B   Working together often leads to a solution.

   C   It is easy to forget numbers.

   D   Old age leads to forgetfulness.

64. Which of the following descriptions does *not* show that the story takes place near a body of water?

   A   "Overhead, seagulls squawked."

   B   "She worked until the sun slipped by a nearby island."

   C   "Once the wind came up and foam started frosting the sea, I gave up and went home."

   D   "Her brow was knit in concentration as she spun the lock's numbers."

65. How can you infer the meaning of the word "marina"?

   A   because the author gives context clues within the story

   B   because the author includes a glossary of terms at the end of the story

   C   because there is an illustration of a marina in the passage

   D   because one of the characters in the story gives its meaning

End

PRACTICE TEST #2

INTRODUCTION TO PRACTICE TEST #2

Now that you've finished the lessons and the first practice test, you're almost done! It's a good time to check your answers to the first practice test, starting on page 185. All of the answers have explanations from pages 186 to 196.

When you are ready, it's time to take the second practice test. The practice tests in this book are similar to the North Carolina EOG Test in Reading for fifth grade.

On the actual EOG Test in Reading, you will answer the questions on a separate sheet of paper. This sheet is called a "Bubble Sheet" because you have to "bubble" in your answers with a pencil.

The bubble sheet for the second practice test is on the next page. You should tear out the bubble sheet or cut it out with a pair of scissors.

Try to take the practice test as if it were the actual test. That means you should follow all the test-taking rules and instructions. Fill in the bubble sheet, and take the entire test at one time. Don't watch television or listen to music when you take the practice test.

Remember to use the tips and lessons you have learned and practiced in this book. They will help you to do your best. After you have taken the test, have an adult go over it. The answers and explanations to the second practice test begins on page 197. Find the areas where you need to practice more and review those lessons again.

Good luck!

PRACTICE TEST #2 ANSWER SHEET

Completely darken bubbles with a No. 2 pencil. If you make a mistake, be sure to erase mark completely. Erase all stray marks.

1. YOUR NAME: _____
(Print) Last   First   M.I.

SIGNATURE: _____   **DATE:** _____ / _____ / _____

HOME ADDRESS: _____
(Print)   Number

_____
City   State   Zip Code

PHONE NO.: _____
(Print)

2. YOUR NAME

First 4 letters of last name				FIRST INIT	MID INIT
A	A	A	A	A	A
B	B	B	B	B	B
C	C	C	C	C	C
D	D	D	D	D	D
E	E	E	E	E	E
F	F	F	F	F	F
G	G	G	G	G	G
H	H	H	H	H	H
I	I	I	I	I	I
J	J	J	J	J	J
K	K	K	K	K	K
L	L	L	L	L	L
M	M	M	M	M	M
N	N	N	N	N	N
O	O	O	O	O	O
P	P	P	P	P	P
Q	Q	Q	Q	Q	Q
R	R	R	R	R	R
S	S	S	S	S	S
T	T	T	T	T	T
U	U	U	U	U	U
V	V	V	V	V	V
W	W	W	W	W	W
X	X	X	X	X	X
Y	Y	Y	Y	Y	Y
Z	Z	Z	Z	Z	Z

3. DATE OF BIRTH

Month	Day	Year
JAN		
FEB		
MAR	0 0	0 0
APR	1 1	1 1
MAY	2 2	2 2
JUN	3 3	3 3
JUL	4 4	4
AUG	5 5	5
SEP	7 7	7
OCT	8 8	8
NOV	9 9	9
DEC		

4. SEX

○ MALE
○ FEMALE

The Princeton Review

Practice Test 2

1. A B C D
2. A B C D
3. A B C D
4. A B C D
5. A B C D
6. A B C D
7. A B C D
8. A B C D
9. A B C D
10. A B C D
11. A B C D
12. A B C D
13. A B C D

14. A B C D
15. A B C D
16. A B C D
17. A B C D
18. A B C D
19. A B C D
20. A B C D
21. A B C D
22. A B C D
23. A B C D
24. A B C D
25. A B C D
26. A B C D

27. A B C D
28. A B C D
29. A B C D
30. A B C D
31. A B C D
32. A B C D
33. A B C D
34. A B C D
35. A B C D
36. A B C D
37. A B C D
38. A B C D
39. A B C D

40. A B C D
41. A B C D
42. A B C D
43. A B C D
44. A B C D
45. A B C D
46. A B C D
47. A B C D
48. A B C D
49. A B C D
50. A B C D
51. A B C D
52. A B C D

53. A B C D
54. A B C D
55. A B C D
56. A B C D
57. A B C D
58. A B C D
59. A B C D
60. A B C D
61. A B C D
62. A B C D
63. A B C D
64. A B C D
65. A B C D

NORTH CAROLINA READING PRACTICE TEST #2

A Passing Train

As the train passes through the sleepy town

The bell chimes ten

And you can hear people passing in the street

Calling out, "Good night dear friend."

Sample 1   When does this poem take place?

    A   in the morning

    B   at noon

    C   in the evening

    D   in the afternoon

Sample 2   If you wanted to read another passage like this one, where would you look?

    A   in an encyclopedia

    B   in a storybook

    C   in a dictionary

    D   in a book of poems

Go to next page

Molly the Inventor

It takes imagination, commitment, and brainpower to be an inventor. Read the following passage about ten-year-old Molly who has been inventing things since she was three years old.

Molly is always thinking. When she comes across an obstacle in the world, she applies her imagination to the problem and figures out a way around it. She is a true inventor.

At ten years old, Molly is already an old hand at inventing. She has been coming up with ways to make life easier and more fun since she was three!

Molly's earliest invention was the snout for a lizard costume. "It is neat when you end up making costumes," Molly says. "It's fun to play in them because it feels like you are an animal. You get the feeling of having a tail and claws."

The Carbonated Drink Squirt Stopper is another example of Molly's ingenuity. Molly invented it after watching her mom get soda all over her clothes when she opened a bottle. Molly went into the laboratory and came up with the "Carbonated Drink Squirt Stopper," or CDSS, a cup that fits around the top of a bottle to catch the fizz when it's opened. Molly entered the CDSS in the competition at the Invention Convention and won second place.

Molly was on a roll. She invented the "Free Hand Umbrella," a knapsack with an umbrella attached to it. She won third place at the Invention Convention with this clever device.

Next Molly noticed that when she put her straw in a drink it pops up and floats. She developed a way to weigh down the straw so that it stays at the bottom of the glass. It may seem simple, but nobody else had ever thought of it! Molly took first prize at the Invention Convention for this innovation. The "Straw Sinker" is Molly's most recent invention, but it is certainly not her last!

Go to next page

1. When the passage says, "She has been coming up with ways to make life easier and more fun since she was three!" what does the author want you to feel about Molly?

    A   confused

    B   irritated

    C   amused

    D   impressed

2. Why is Molly called an "old hand" at inventing?

    A   She likes dressing up in costumes.

    B   She invented an umbrella that you don't have to carry.

    C   She has been inventing things since she was young.

    D   She uses her hands when she invents things.

3. Which of the following words **best** characterizes Molly?

    A   greedy

    B   creative

    C   sophisticated

    D   insecure

4. What is the **best** way to complete the web?

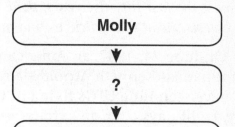

    A   costumes

    B   mathematical abilities

    C   inventions

    D   soda

5. What would be the **best** book to read if you wanted to find out more about Molly?

    A   a book on recent inventions

    B   a book on rain clouds

    C   a book on money

    D   a book on geniuses

Go to next page

UFOs: Real or Fiction?

For almost the last fifty-five years, there have been reports of encounters with unidentified flying objects. Read this article to find out what the experts think.

On June 24, 1947, an American pilot named Kenneth Arnold claimed to have seen nine UFOs flying in the sky. Eight days later, an extraterrestrial spacecraft allegedly crashed in Roswell, New Mexico. As a result of the crash, the U.S. government and UFO enthusiasts spent the next thirty years trying to determine whether the debris from the crash belonged to some of kind spaceship. In 1994, the Air Force issued a report claiming that the debris was from a balloon that had been launched in 1947 as part of an experiment.

The Roswell incident, as it is referred to, was the first reported UFO sighting, but it has not been the last. On June 5, 1969, several crewmembers on an American Airlines flight flying near St. Louis reported seeing several unidentified flying objects. They were "flying in a square formation" according to the FAA controller who was sitting in the cockpit. Shaped like hydroplanes, the largest appeared to be about eighteen to twenty feet long and seven to eight feet thick. They were "burnished aluminum" the controller said, and long streams of blue-green flames trailed behind them.

Were the objects really spaceships? The sighting happened to coincide with a giant meteor, called the Iowa Fireball, falling from the sky. Experts believe the pilots could have mistaken the meteor for a UFO. However, that hardly closes the case on UFOs. Some experts believe that UFOs are real, but that people are afraid to admit they've seen them because, according to John Mack, a Harvard University psychiatrist, it's socially unacceptable. "I've interviewed airline pilots who have had sightings—close up sightings of UFOs," he said. "They will not report it, because they will be removed from their work."

Other scientists, like Carl Sagan, say there is still no real proof. "The fact that someone says something doesn't mean that it's true." Sagan continued:

"To be taken seriously, you need physical evidence that can be examined at leisure by skeptical scientists: a scraping of the whole ship, and the discovery that it contains isotopic ratios that aren't present on Earth . . . or materials of absolutely bizarre properties of many sorts. . . . But there's no scrapings, no interior photographs, no filched page from the captain's log book. All there are are stories."

No doubt, as long as UFO sightings continue, scientists will keep debating whether they are real or not.

Go to next page

6. What is the **best** thing to do, before you begin reading, to increase your understanding the passage?

    A   Ask an adult to summarize the passage for you.

    B   Circle all of the words that you don't understand.

    C   Count the number of words in the passage.

    D   Skim the title, introduction, and first paragraph to find the main idea of the passage.

7. Which information in the passage suggests that the objects observed by the American Airlines crewmembers were **not** UFOs?

    A   the remarks made by John Mack

    B   the unreliability of the controller

    C   the sighting of a meteor at the same time

    D   the burnished aluminum color of the spaceship

8. The first reported UFO sighting in the passage was observed by whom?

    A   John Mack

    B   an American Airlines pilot

    C   Kenneth Arnold

    D   Carl Sagan

9. Why is the selection indented after the fourth paragraph?

    A   There is an excerpt from a speech.

    B   The indented text is the proof that UFOs don't exist.

    C   The text there is the most important part of the passage.

    D   The indented text is the continuation of a quote from Carl Sagan.

10. Where would you look to find **current** information on UFOs?

    A   a magazine from 1947 about the Roswell incident

    B   an almanac

    C   a book

    D   a dictionary

11. Which of the following topics is **most** related to this passage?

    A   mysteries of space

    B   history of airplanes

    C   interesting scientific facts

    D   bizarre experiences

Go to next page

Cooking

What kind of cook are you? If you are interested in cooking, this is just the article for you to read. You'll learn some secrets for improving your performance in the kitchen.

Do you like eating? Have you ever felt your stomach rumble, opened the refrigerator, and felt disappointed?

You should learn to cook. As long as your kitchen has a few basic ingredients, you can make many yummy meals and snacks.

Learning how to cook will improve your life. You will impress your friends by making tasty, after-school snacks. You can surprise your parents by bringing them breakfast in bed.

Cooking is an art that takes many years to master. Many chefs are graduates of professional cooking schools. There, they learn to chop vegetables or make a perfect sauce.

However, knowing a few simple tricks can be enough to make anyone comfortable in the kitchen. "Start out with easy recipes," recommends cooking teacher Daniela Chin. "In fact, there are a lot of things you can make without a recipe."

After running her own restaurant, Chin began offering cooking classes to young people. She teaches about the chemistry of cooking. She also teaches practical skills, such as the differences between paprika and chili powder or a teaspoon and a tablespoon.

As you become a better cook, you'll be able to read a recipe and know how it will taste. You'll even see ways of experimenting with it.

Gaining more experience will also allow you to cook without a recipe. Cooking is a creative art. Chefs constantly invent new recipes based on the freshest food that is available. If lobster and asparagus are in season, they might find a way to combine them. The more you know about food and flavors, the more creative you can be.

Here are two tips to help you cook.

Fresh Ingredients: The foundation of good food is fresh ingredients. Buy fruits and vegetables when they are in season. Then make sure you treat them well. For example, wash your lettuce immediately after bringing it home. Make sure you've dried it thoroughly before placing it in a plastic bag for storage.

Stay Simple: If you buy the best ingredients, prepare them simply. Their natural flavors will outshine fancy preparation. Buy garden fresh tomatoes. Instead of turning the tomatoes into a salad, simply drizzle them with olive oil and light salt. This will allow you to appreciate their natural sweetness.

Learning the fundamentals of cooking will allow you to move on to more complicated combinations.

Go to next page

12. Which of the following issues is **not** addressed in the passage?

A   What is the best way to store lettuce?

B   What is the difference between paprika and chili powder?

C   How can cooking be creative?

D   Why is it important to prepare food simply?

13. The passage mentions all of the following things as reasons for learning to cook **except** for which one?

A   You can experiment and invent your own recipes.

B   You can impress your friends.

C   You can earn a lot of money as a chef.

D   You can satisfy your craving for good food.

14. Why did the author include two tips in the article?

A   to give readers easy suggestions for becoming better cooks

B   to show how easy it is to become a chef

C   to demonstrate creative ways to format articles

D   to prove that fresh ingredients improve all dishes

15. Why are buying fresh ingredients and staying simple important first steps for beginning cooks?

A   They are the basis for making fancy sauces.

B   They teach cooks how to read recipes.

C   They help cooks recognize the natural goodness of food.

D   They allow cooks to experiment.

16. The **main** idea of this passage is best expressed by which answer choice below?

A   Cooking well is a creative way to enhance your life.

B   Eating at good restaurants will help you learn to cook.

C   Becoming a professional chef is the only way to learn the basics.

D   Being creative helps you read recipes.

17. Why did the author interview cooking teacher Daniela Chin for this article?

A   to impress the reader

B   to learn about becoming a professional chef

C   to make the passage more varied

D   to get comments from an expert

Go to next page

Sound

When you hear a sound, what causes it? And how is it formed? Read the following passage to find out.

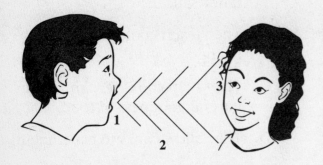

Sounds result when something moves, disturbing the air, ground, or water around it. The sound moves in vibrating waves from the source of the disturbance. Here's how it works.

1. When you speak, you push and vibrate the air molecules out of your mouth in a straight line. These molecules disturb the molecules next to them and so on. This is the way sound travels. The molecules vibrate, moving back and forth, disturbing other molecules around them. The energy from the sound of the word travels through a row of molecules.

2. Sound waves need particles of matter (molecules) in order to exist. Without molecules, sound waves would have nothing to disturb, and there would be no sound. That's why there is no sound in space!

3. Our ears can detect sound waves vibrating between 20 and 20,000 waves per second. If it is vibrating below 20 waves per second, it is called subsonic. If it is vibrating above 20,000 waves per second, it is known as ultrasonic.

Go to next page

18. Why did the author use parentheses in the second point?

    A   to give the Latin word

    B   to provide an abbreviation

    C   to define a common word

    D   to offer the scientific term

19. What does sound depend on?

    A   loud noises

    B   particles of matter

    C   vocal cords

    D   air

20. Which of the following is the *most* important reason for including the picture?

    A   to make the passage faster to read

    B   to teach how sound travels

    C   to indicate how quickly sound travels

    D   to show the density of sound waves

21. How could you find further information about sound?

    A   by listening carefully to your teacher

    B   by reading a book about music

    C   by going to a rock concert

    D   by reading a scientific article on hearing

22. If you didn't understand the word "vibrating," what could you do *first*?

    A   Look up its meaning in a dictionary.

    B   Write down the word and ask your teacher for the definition.

    C   See if the word is defined within the text.

    D   Skip the word and move on to the next sentence.

Go to next page

The Journey of Meng Chiang-nu

China has an ancient storytelling tradition. Some Chinese myths and folktales come from the period of the Han Dynasty, which existed between 200 B.C. and A.D. 200. Read the following passage, a Han folktale, to learn what happened because of Meng Chiang-nu's love for her husband Wan Hsi-liang.

During the Chin dynasty, the cruel emperor Shih Huang decided to build a Great Wall to protect his empire from invasion. He ordered his subjects to come from across the land to build the wall. Toiling day and night, they carried heavy earth and bricks, they ate little, and their clothes became thin and ragged.

Wan Hsi-liang was living a happy life with his beautiful and faithful wife Meng Chiang-nu before he was called to help build the Great Wall. For many weeks after he left, Meng Chiang-nu heard no news of her husband. She was consumed with apprehension. Winter melted into spring. The flowers bloomed, the trees grew buds, and the clouds were high in the blue sky. Birds sang happy melodies. All this cheerfulness only served to make Meng Chiang-nu feel her sadness more deeply, because she could not share it with Wan Hsi-liang. Spring eventually turned to autumn. As the weather turned cold, Meng Chiang-nu made Wan Hsi-liang some clothes lined with layers of padded cotton to keep him warm. Because she had no other way to get the clothes to him, she resolved to take them herself. This took great courage, because Meng Chiang-nu had never ventured far from home before.

Meng Chiang-nu set off for the wall, walking day after day after day.

One night, overcome with fatigue, she took shelter in a tiny stone temple at the roadside. As soon as she lay down, she fell fast asleep, and no sooner was she asleep then she dreamed of Wan Hsi-liang. He came toward her, his arms outstretched, and Meng Chiang-nu felt warm and comforted. Then Wan Hsi-liang told her that he had died. Meng Chiang-nu woke up very upset. She cursed the emperor who had taken her husband from her and made so many people's lives miserable. Then she resumed her journey.

Along the way, Meng Chiang-nu endured many hardships. One day she woke up covered in a sheet of snow. Another day she became quite lost. A crow landed on the ground before her, cawed several times, flew a short distance off, then landed in front of her again. The crow was showing her the way to go, and she followed it. One day Meng Chiang-nu came over a mountain pass. Before her a high stone wall snaked over hills and mountains as far as she could see. She had reached the Great Wall. She was so excited that she immediately began asking people if they knew her husband. No one had heard of him. Meng Chiang-nu saw people so skinny that their bones poked out through their threadbare clothes. Finally, she met a man who had

Go to next page

Roadmap to 5th Grade Reading: North Carolina Edition

known her husband. He told her that Wan Hsi-liang had died, and his fellow workers put him in the earth beneath the Great Wall.

Meng Chiang-nu began to cry and wept for many days. Her sorrow was so deep it touched the hearts of the workers, and they began to cry with her. Soon the tears and the wails brought on a raging storm. The storm picked up bricks and dirt off the Great Wall. When the storm finally passed, more than two hundred miles of the Great Wall had collapsed. The people along the wall were awestruck, for they realized that Meng Chiang-nu's bitter sorrow had caused the wall to come down. In their hearts, they harbored secret gladness that the emperor's project had been destroyed.

The emperor heard about the crumbled wall and came to see for himself, determined to punish whoever was responsible. When he saw Meng Chiang-nu, however, he was so taken with her grace and beauty that instead of punishing her, he asked her to be his wife. Meng Chiang-nu agreed to marry him if he agreed to bury Wan Hsi-liang in a lavish gold coffin with a silver lid. She also demanded the emperor must himself attend the funeral, showing humility before her husband's grave.

Anxious to make Meng Chiang-nu his wife, the emperor fulfilled all her wishes. The funeral march proceeded down to the edge of a flowing river. Meng Chiang-nu knelt before her husband's grave. Then, quick as a blink, she flung herself into the river. She had no intention of marrying the emperor. The emperor flew into a rage. He was not used to being disobeyed. He commanded his assistants to pull Meng Chiang-nu from the river. Just when they got near her, Meng Chiang-nu transformed into a lovely multi-colored fish. She slipped easily from the men's grasp and swam away with ease and grace, following the river to the an undersea world that was peaceful and free.

23. Why does Meng Chaing-nu throw herself into the river?

   A She does not want to marry the emperor.

   B She is transformed into a beautiful fish.

   C She wants to destroy the Great Wall.

   D Her husband's lavish coffin is taken to the river's edge.

24. Meng Chiang-nu's feelings during her search for her husband can be described by all of the following *except* for which adjective?

   A angry

   B exhausted

   C optimistic

   D lost

Go to next page

25. How does Meng Chiang-nu manage to have her husband buried properly?

   A   She causes the wall to fall down.

   B   She dreams her husband is dead.

   C   She follows a crow.

   D   She tricks the emperor.

26. Why does Wan Hsi-liang leave his wife?

   A   He is ordered by the emperor to help construct a great wall.

   B   He is looking for his sister.

   C   He is being punished for loving her too much.

   D   He wants to protect the empire from invasion.

27. Which is the *best* description of the people's response to the crumbling of the great wall?

   A   outraged but joyful

   B   tired but saddened

   C   disturbed but energetic

   D   shocked but happy

28. How does the story's author make the story surprising?

   A   by summarizing the history of China

   B   by giving Meng Chiang-nu magical powers

   C   by describing Meng Chiang-nu's journey

   D   by explaining the construction of the Great Wall

29. When the story says that Meng Chiang-nu is "consumed with apprehension," what does this mean?

   A   She is starving.

   B   She is understanding.

   C   She is calm.

   D   She is worried.

Go to next page

Roberto Clemente

The great baseball player, Roberto Clemente, traveled far from his home in Puerto Rico to play baseball in America. However, he never forgot his heritage. Read this passage to learn more about his career.

Roberto Clemente was one of the best baseball players of all time, and he never forgot his family or his Puerto Rican heritage. Born on August 18, 1934, in Puerto Rico, Clemente was the youngest of seven children. His father oversaw a sugarcane plantation, and his mother managed a grocery store for the workers.

Clemente admired his parents enormously. "When I was a boy," he said, "I realized what lovely persons my mother and father were. I learned the right way to live."

Part of the right way to live was working hard. Clemente was nine years old when he decided he wanted a bike. He earned the money by delivering milk. For his work, he received only a penny a day. It took him three years to save up enough money to buy the bicycle. "I am from the poor people," he said. "I represent the poor people. I like workers. I like people that suffer because these people have a different approach to life from the people that have everything and don't know what suffering is."

Clemente brought the same work ethic to baseball. He spent many hours improving his skills. Although his father thought it was time for Clemente to give up baseball, the young man continued playing. When he was seventeen, a scout from a professional Puerto Rican baseball team spotted him and asked him to play for their team. His pay was $40 per month, plus a $500 bonus for signing.

Clemente played so well for the Santurce team that he caught the eye of major league scouts looking for new talent. In 1954, he signed with the Brooklyn Dodgers. The following year, after playing in the minor league for a year, he started playing for the Pittsburgh Pirates.

After five years of perfecting his game and getting used to the major league, Clemente exploded on the scene. In 1960, he had a strong batting average. He hit sixteen home runs and brought ninety-four runs in. That year, the Pirates swept the National Pennant and the World Series. For the next twelve years, Clemente wowed fans. He was fast on the field, and he had a powerful arm. He would chase down balls in remote corners of the field, and he often crashed into the outfield walls making incredible catches. He could even throw the ball over four hundred feet to home plate!

At the plate, Clemente was also impressive. He was a "spray hitter," hitting the ball into spaces between the fielders. He left his mark in the baseball history books by becoming the eleventh player to get three thousand hits in his lifetime. In 1971, he received the World Series' outstanding player award.

Go to next page

Clemente didn't allow his success on the field to make him forget his past. He took other Hispanic baseball players under his wing. He opened up his home in Puerto Rico to fans. When he had time, he offered baseball clinics to children all over the island. "I go to different towns, different neighborhoods," he said. "I get kids together and talk about the importance of sports, the importance of being a good citizen, the importance of respecting their mother and father."

Clemente had dreamed his whole life of building a sports complex for Puerto Rican children. In 1972 he planned to retire from baseball and begin planning. Before that, however, a huge earthquake struck Nicaragua. Because of Clemente's commitment to helping the poor, he collected relief supplies in Puerto Rico. He was going to deliver them personally when his plane crashed near San Juan, Puerto Rico. He died in that crash on December 31, 1972. Clemente's dream didn't die, however. His family built a sports complex in his memory.

30. Which of the following is the **best** characterization of Roberto Clemente?

A   arrogant and selfless

B   disciplined and generous

C   fanciful and strange

D   sad and tired

31. How did Clemente give back to his community?

A   Clemente mentored other Hispanic baseball players, both in the professional league and in Puerto Rican communities.

B   Clemente had no energy for anything but baseball.

C   Clemente didn't spend much time in Puerto Rico.

D   Clemente hit very well, and he had one of the most powerful arms in all of baseball history.

32. What conclusion can you draw about Clemente's personality from the sentence, "Clemente didn't allow his success on the field to make him forget his past"?

A   Clemente didn't recognize his present success and lived in the past.

B   Clemente was unable to enjoy his accomplishments.

C   Clemente was a very arrogant man.

D   Clemente's success in baseball didn't interfere with his commitment to Puerto Rico.

Go to next page

33. You might read about Clemente for all of the following reasons *except* for which answer choice?

   A   to prompt you to think about the importance of family and community

   B   to inspire you to work hard no matter how unattainable your goals seem

   C   to teach you how to develop a strong throwing arm

   D   to motivate you to use your gifts to help others

34. Besides being fast on the field, what else was Clemente skilled at?

   A   Clemente hit the most home runs in the league.

   B   Clemente was an overpowering pitcher.

   C   Clemente was recruited to play for the Brooklyn Dodgers.

   D   Clemente was an expert "spray hitter."

35. How is the author trying to make you feel about Clemente?

   A   sad

   B   respectful

   C   offended

   D   confused

36. The author impresses you with Clemente's ability as a baseball player by including all of the following facts *except* for which one?

   A   the amount of Clemente's salary when he played for Pittsburgh

   B   mention of the awards that Clemente won

   C   a description of Clemente's skill on the field

   D   the number of hits Clemente had in his lifetime

37. The *main* idea of this passage is best expressed by which of the following statements?

   A   Honoring your parents is important.

   B   Practice will enable you to become perfect.

   C   Baseball is the great American sport.

   D   Hard work can help you realize your goals, but you should never forget where you began.

Go to next page

Read the following poems and find out how each poet feels about cities.

A London Thoroughfare, 2 A.M. *by Amy Lowell*

They have watered the street,
It shines in the glare of lamps.
Cold, white lamps,
And lies
Like a slow-moving river,
Barred with silver and black.
Cabs go down it,
One, And then another.
Between them I hear the shuffling of
    feet.
Tramps doze on the window ledges,
Nightwalkers pass along the
    sidewalks.
The city is squalid and sinister,
With the silver-barred street in the
    midst,
Slow-moving,
A river leading nowhere.
Opposite my window,
The moon cuts
Clear and round,
Through the plum-coloured night.
She cannot light the city;
It is too bright.
It has white lamps,
And glitters coldly.
I stand in the window and watch the
    moon.
She is thin and lustreless,
But I love her.
I know the moon,
And this is an alien city.

City Night *by Stephanie Reents*

Out my window, cabs zip by
And people stroll in merry groups
Neon signs are blinking stars in the
    sky
Though it's night, the city is alive!
Though it's past midnight, I feel
    alive
Watching the cars pass in a lively stream
The streets teem like a productive
    bee hive
Beneath the moon's strong, steady
    beam
This city never sleeps, they say
A man on the corner is selling his
    art
As people take their dogs on strolls
    through the park
The city maintains a twenty-four
    hour day
And for this I say, hurray! Hurray!

Go to next page

38. Which of the following statements most clearly expresses the meaning of "City Night"?

A   Every night, people should gaze out their windows.

B   Many artists sell their work at night.

C   Cities are filled with exciting energy.

D   Getting used to a city's noise and light is difficult.

39. Which word describes the tone of "A London Thoroughfare, 2 A.M."?

A   celebratory

B   tired

C   gloomy

D   unclear

40. In the first stanza of "City Night" which lines rhyme?

A   the first and second

B   the first and third

C   the first and fourth

D   the second and third

41. What is the meaning of the word "squalid" in "A London Thoroughfare, 2 A.M."?

A   lively

B   miserable

C   beautiful

D   confusing

Go to next page

42. The word "alive" is repeated twice in "City Night" for all of the following reasons *except* for which one?

   A   to connect the speaker to the city

   B   to create rhythm through repetition

   C   to indicate why the speaker is still awake

   D   to emphasize the feeling of liveliness

43. What is the *best* approach to reading a poem for its meaning?

   A   ignore any figurative language that you don't understand

   B   read slowly and summarize the meaning at the end of each line

   C   read each line forward, then backward

   D   try to guess what the poem is about

44. What is the *main* similarity between "A London Thoroughfare, 2 A.M." and "City Night"?

   A   Both describe cities at night.

   B   Both include rivers flowing through the city.

   C   Both focus on the colors of the city.

   D   Both depict people walking their dogs.

45. In what way does the moon in the first poem have a different meaning than the moon in the second?

   A   It is thin and lustreless.

   B   It represents the city's aggressiveness and unnaturalness.

   C   It overpowers the city lights.

   D   It happily lights the night activities.

Go to next page

Making Papier Mâché Masks

Have you ever made your own mask? This craft project will tell you how to do it.

Materials

Newspaper

Papier mâché paste*

Wax paper

Tinfoil

Paint

*Papier Mâché Paste: Mix two cups of flour with four cups of water. The mixture should be the consistency of glue. If it is too thick, add additional water. If it is too thin, add additional flour. Stir until the paste is smooth. Add a few pinches of salt.

1. Cover the table you are going to work on with newspaper. Place wax paper over the newspaper. This will help you keep things tidier.

2. With the help of a friend or parent, place a double-thick layer of tinfoil on your face. Gently press the tinfoil around your forehead, eyes, nose, mouth, and cheeks. You are making a mold of your face.

3. After you have finished molding the tinfoil to your face, carefully remove it. Crumple up some newspaper and place it on the inside of the mold. This will help the mold keep its shape.

4. Tear newspaper into strips. They should be one inch wide and six to eight inches long.

5. Dip a strip of newspaper into the paste you made earlier. Place it very gently on your mask. If you press too hard, you'll change the shape of your mask and you won't recognize yourself. Continue until you've covered the mask. Then, set aside the mask to allow it to dry.

6. Cover your mask in at least two more layers of papier mâché. Make sure that each layer dries completely before you add the next one.

7. When you are finished, paint your mask. Make sure you make some small breathing holes for your nostrils and mouth.

8. Clean up the sticky bowl of paste. (Lots of hot water will do the trick.) Recycle the leftover newspaper and wipe up any spills. Now you can model your beautiful mask for your friends.

Go to next page

46. To make doing this craft project easier, what could be changed about the directions?

    A write the directions in larger print

    B list the paste ingredients under "Materials"

    C explain the history of masks

    D include a picture of a completed mask

47. Newspaper is placed behind the tinfoil mold for which purpose?

    A to make the mold appear more like a head

    B to prevent the paste from dripping

    C to make the mold heavier

    D to prevent the mold from being crushed

48. What can you use to decorate a mask?

    A newspaper

    B paint

    C make-up

    D tinfoil

49. The following items are needed for this project *except* for which one?

    A newspaper

    B flour

    C glue

    D tinfoil

50. Which is the first step in making this mask?

    A make a mold of your face

    B paint the mask

    C tear newspaper into strips

    D allow the mask to dry

51. To complete this project, which is the *best* way to read the instructions?

    A Read a step, then complete it, until reaching the end.

    B Memorize the list of materials before reading further.

    C Read the whole passage briefly, and then go back and read each step carefully before you begin it.

    D Read every other step, then read all of them in order.

Go to next page

Hector Henry's Haunted House

Hector Henry is always getting himself in trouble because of his overactive imagination. Read this story about what happened to him when he visited the attic.

Hector Henry was staying home alone and he was supposed to clean his cluttered room before his parents returned from the movies.

Before getting started, however, he decided to explore the attic, where his parents stored mementos (keepsakes or objects that people treasure and keep to remind them of the past) from their childhoods, and climbed up the creaky ladder.

When he opened the door to the dim, musty attic, he saw a sight that almost made his blood curdle; it was a pale white ghost, hovering in front of the windows and looking out to the street below. As quick as lightning, he slammed the door and bolted back down the stairs.

What was Hector Henry going to do? How could he stay in the house knowing a ghost inhabited it?

He called his friend Ziad Chomsky, who offered to come over immediately and keep him company. Once Ziad arrived, the two boys paced back and forth while listening for the slightest strange sound.

It was a terrifying situation knowing that his house was haunted, and Hector Henry collapsed on the couch in exhaustion. Ziad tried to comfort him by suggesting that they call the police because the ghost was technically an intruder.

Hector Henry didn't know what to do. If they called the police, they would have to return to the attic, and if they returned to the attic, he might see the ghost again. He turned white imagining the ghost. He didn't want to call the police, but he also didn't want to live with the ghost.

Time crawled by, but at last he heard the sound of his parents' car pulling into the driveway. As soon as they walked through the door, he blurted out his story.

His parents shook their heads. "Why didn't you just go over to Ziad's house?"

"And leave the ghost in the house alone?" he answered.

His father went up to attic immediately, and when he returned he announced he had found nothing. Hector had probably mistaken the thin white curtains for a ghost.

"Next time, you're going to have to think of a better excuse for not cleaning your room," his mother said, laughing. "Seeing an imaginary ghost is not enough to keep you out of hot water."

Go to next page

52. Why doesn't Hector Henry clean his room?

    A   He is supposed to move his old toys to the attic.

    B   Ziad comes over and distracts him.

    C   He is too busy exploring the attic.

    D   He becomes too terrified to think of cleaning his room.

53. Who does Ziad propose calling to solve the problem?

    A   the police

    B   his parents

    C   Hector Henry's parents

    D   the neighbors

54. The author's **main** objective in writing this story is which of the following?

    A   to judge

    B   to teach

    C   to entertain

    D   to terrify

55. How does the author reveal the definition of the word "mementos"?

    A   by placing the definition in parentheses

    B   by offering contextual clues

    C   by defining the word in a footnote

    D   by italicizing the word

56. Which of the following describes Hector Henry's reaction to the ghost?

    A   making the best of a difficult time

    B   being paralyzed with fear

    C   learning an important lesson

    D   seeing things that aren't real

57. All of the following descriptions show the reader how scared Hector Henry is **except** for which one?

    A   " . . . he saw a sight that almost made his blood curdle."

    B   " . . . he slammed the door and bolted back down the stairs."

    C   "he . . . climbed up the creaky ladder."

    D   " . . . he collapsed on the couch in exhaustion."

Go to next page

Island Life

The following selection is from a story written by a girl who lives on an island. It describes what life is like for her. As you read it, think about how your life is different from hers.

I live on an island called Obstruction. It is off the coast of Washington. Living here is very different from living in a typical town or city.

Living on an island is a unique experience, especially an island like ours. Obstruction is a dry island. That means there are not any lakes or rivers. Behind our house is a well that supplies us with water. The well water is limited, so we also have rain barrels that collect water when it rains. We use this water for bathing, washing things, and watering our garden.

My father built our house. It is three stories tall, and it looks out on the ocean. Because we don't have electricity, we heat our house with a wood-burning stove. One of my jobs is to help my father chop wood. It's hard work, but it gives me a sense of satisfaction to see the wood stacked up high and to know that we have enough fuel for the winter.

Luckily, we also have a diesel generator. When we turn on the generator, we can turn on lights, and I can use my computer. Unfortunately, we don't have access to the Internet. Do you know why? It's because we don't have a regular phone. That's strange, isn't it?

The other strange thing is that there is no grocery store on Obstruction. We have to sail our boat to another island to buy food. As you can imagine, we buy huge quantities of supplies. It's no fun to run out of milk or bread when the store is a boat ride away. We also have a gigantic garden. In the summer, we grow so many fruits and vegetables—such as lettuce, cucumbers, tomatoes, and zucchini—that we can barely eat them all. This year, I'm trying to grow a huge pumpkin that I want to enter in the county fair.

There are twelve other houses on Obstruction, but we're the only people who live on the island year-round. The other families use their houses during the summer. As you can imagine, summer is my favorite season. Then, there are many other children for me to play with.

My friends and I do all sorts of fun things. Sometimes, we explore the island. Because it's small, we can go wherever we want. My friend Jenny and I like to follow the deer paths to the blackberry bushes in the center of the island. In August, when the berries get fat and ripe, we pick buckets of blackberries and make blackberry pie.

We also like to dig for clams. To do this, we first read the tide charts to find out when there will be a low tide and more of the beach will be exposed. Then, we head down to the beach with our shovels and buckets. The clams are buried in the sand, but

Go to next page

they send up little streams of water. We dig in the spots where we see spurts. The best kinds of clams are steamers. They're small and thin, and they have beige colored shells. Gooey ducks are another type of clam. They're fatter, and they have fat necks.

Of course, we always have to visit the tide pools at the north end of our beach. Tide pools are left behind when the tide goes out. Water is trapped behind rocks along with all kinds of interesting sea creatures such as starfish, jellyfish, and sea anemones. Once Jenny and I saw an octopus. That was a scary sight! Its eight arms were covered in suction cups.

Oh, you're probably wondering whether I go to school. Of course! Except instead of walking or hopping on a school bus, I hop on the school boat. It's a little motor boat that picks up children from all the small islands and takes them to Orcas. Once we dock at Orcas, I ride a school bus. When I get a little older, my dad says I can kayak to school on sunny days. I can hardly wait for that!

58. Why does the author's family collect water in rain barrels?

    A It is cleaner than the water in the well.

    B They want to keep the well from running dry.

    C It quenches their thirst.

    D They don't have a well, so it's their only source of water.

59. Which adjective *best* describes the author's feelings about living on an island?

    A normal

    B envious

    C angry

    D special

60. Which is the *best* way to fill in the graphic organizer?

Island Life vs. Mainland Life	
Differences	
Island Life	**Mainland Life**
• ?	• water from a faucet
• heat from a wood-burning stove	• gas or electric furnace
• electricity from a generator	• electricity from a power plant
• no year-round neighbors	• many neighbors
• school boat	• school bus

    A bathtub

    B water from a well

    C old-fashioned plumbing

    D natural water

Go to next page

61. What clues suggest that this passage could be autobiographical?

    A   It tells about one person's life from his or her point of view.

    B   It describes unusual circumstances.

    C   It is about contemporary life.

    D   It includes fictional events.

62. After reading the passage, you know that all of the following are differences between living on an island and living on the mainland *except* for which one?

    A   communication

    B   transportation

    C   friendships

    D   grocery shopping

63. Which book would be *least* helpful in finding information on living on islands?

    A   a reference book on island communities

    B   a tale about being shipwrecked on an island

    C   an autobiography about growing up on an island off the coast of Maine

    D   a cookbook filled with seafood recipes

64. What is the purpose of reading this passage?

    A   to imagine how life is different on an island

    B   to explore the hardships of living without electricity

    C   to learn how to grow huge pumpkins

    D   to find out the best kind of clams to eat

65. The author made this passage fun to read by including all of the following elements *except* for which one?

    A   the narrator's favorite activities

    B   how island life is different from the lives many lead

    C   the lakes and rivers of the island

    D   a casual style of writing

End

LESSON ANSWER KEY

LESSON ANSWER KEY

Mile 1: Before Reading

A. Stories about animals

B. Information on the bus schedule

C. Information about a volcanic eruption

D. Information about skits to do at birthday parties

E. Information about scientific discoveries

F. Poems about animals

G. Information on Florida

H. Stories about young people who play chess

I. A story about Eliza

J. Information about treasures in the ocean

K. Nursery rhymes

L. Instructions for craft projects

The book entitled <u>Amazing Animal Facts</u> is nonfiction.

The book entitled <u>Fantastic Animal Stories</u> is fiction.

1. Nonfiction

2. Fiction

3. Fiction

4. Fiction

5. Nonfiction

6. Fiction

7. Nonfiction

8. Fiction

9. Nonfiction

10. Fiction

Any true statements (nonfiction) about animals would be correct for 11. Below are two examples.

11. Kangaroos are native to Australia.

    Pandas are an endangered species.

Any made-up statements (fiction) about animals would be correct for 12. Below are two examples.

12. Kathy the kangaroo wanted nothing more than to move to America.

    Peter the panda paid a person to paddle to Pennsylvania.

Mile 2: Why Do People Read?

To have fun:

Fairy Tales

Plays

Poems

Myths

Humorous Stories

To gain knowledge:

Autobiographies

Biographies

Maps

Newspaper Articles

Magazine Articles

Encyclopedia Articles

Schedules

Scientific Illustrations

Weather Reports

Dictionary Definitions

History Textbook

To learn how to do things:

Recipes

Art Projects

Science Experiments

Directions

1. a history book

2. A person might read this selection to find out more information about Gandhi.

3. a schedule

4. A person might read this selection to find out when the bus leaves.

5. an encyclopedia article

6. A person might read this selection to learn more about treasure hunting.

7. a poem

8. A person might read this selection for the enjoyment of reading a poem.

9. a story

10. A person might read this selection to have fun reading a scary story.

Mile 3 : How Do People Read?

1. Go to a quiet, comfortable place to read.

2. Read the titles and heading in the assignment.

3. Decide the purpose of the reading assignment.

4. Read the selection.

5. Reread the parts of the assignment that you had trouble with and use context clues to figure them out.

6. Think about and summarize what you've read.

7. Use the dictionary, the library, or the Internet to learn more about what you've read.

Map Check 1

1. C	7. C
2. A	8. A
3. B	9. C
4. D	10. C
5. C	11. A
6. C	12. D

Mile 4: Finding the Main Idea

1. Dom missed having waffles for breakfast because he slept too late.

2. Oceans are saltier than rivers for several reasons.

3. Juanita received a big surprise on her birthday.

4. There are many different symptoms of dehydration.

5. Frederick Douglass had a difficult life. He was born a slave, and he worked hard to win his freedom. After he was free, he tried to help other slaves win their freedom.

6. The famous author and champion of the rights of African Americans and women traveled a long way from his humble beginnings.

Mile 5: Finding Supporting Ideas

The supporting details listed below show only some of many possible answers. Any response that lists a supporting detail to the main idea would be correct.

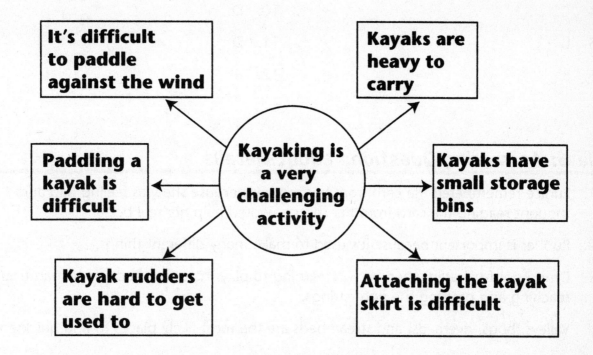

Map Check 2

1. A	7. A
2. D	8. C
3. D	9. C
4. C	10. D
5. D	11. D
6. B	12. B

Mile 6: Answering Questions about Details

1. Eunice remembered the card from her mother because she was feeling bad and thought reading the card from her mother would help her feel better.

2. Rubber is important because it's used to make many different things.

3. Dmitri got frustrated when he was learning to play the guitar because he had trouble reaching and pressing the right strings.

4. Valleys, bogs, riverbeds, and streambeds are the most likely places to find quicksand.

Mile 7: Learning Vocabulary in Context

The following words should be matched

mannerisms ———> habits

identical ———> exactly alike

genetic material ———> chemical molecules

heredity ———> inherited

environmental ———> circumstances

traits ———> characteristics

Map Check 3

1. A
2. C
3. D
4. B
5. B
6. A
7. C

8. A
9. D
10. C
11. C
12. D
13. B
14. C

Mile 8: Making Predictions

You can make different predictions, as long as they made sense with the story.

1. The story will be about a boy who always goes first. Perhaps, he'll still be first at the end of the story, or he won't be able to be first at the end of the story.

2. When they're captains, Cassius and Abel won't choose Ugali for their kickball teams.

3. Ugali will learn that he doesn't always get to be first all the time.

4. At first, I thought the story could either be about Ugali going first or not going first. Now, it seems it will be about him not going first.

5. I found out that Cassius and Abel don't like Ugali, and that they plan to not choose him for their kickball teams.

6. Ugali doesn't get chosen first for the kickball team. Instead of becoming a nicer person, he begins playing tetherball all by himself.

7. I thought Ugali would learn to be second, third or even last. I had no idea that Ugali would start playing tetherball. I was surprised that he becomes so unpopular by the end of the story.

Mile 9: Drawing Conclusions

There are no right or wrong answers for this question. You could have written anything that is shown in the picture. Below are six examples, even though you only needed four.

1. It's a hot day, and the players are trying to stay cool.

2. Some kids are playing a baseball game.

3. The girl with the braids hit the ball to outfield.

4. Instead of retrieving the ball, the outfielder is petting a cat.

5. The coach is very angry.

6. The coach is angry at the outfielder who is not paying attention.

---

1. The woman is a cowgirl. She's going to ride her horse at the county fair.

2. The little boy just lost his balloon. He is very upset.

3. The young woman is dressed up. She's bringing a pie for the food competition.

4. The man is an entertainer. He eats fire.

5. The man is a farmer. He is bringing chickens to the fair.

6. The woman is a chef. She is going to sell scones at the fair.

7. The man is a businessman. He is feeling hot and annoyed.

8. The kids are happy to be buying tickets to the fair. They have many coins.

---

1. She feels very scared and nervous.

2. She feels afraid of the pig because it is gross and seems dangerous.

3. Tali would feel disgusted if the pig rolled over on her. She would probably throw up.

4. Tali is singing the song in hopes of drawing someone's attention and getting help to escape from the pig.

5. She doesn't want to wake up the pig.

Mile 10: Drawing Conclusions about Authors' Choices

1. The author has made this story enjoyable to read by providing details about how Basil feels about the ocean and the forest. It is also enjoyable because it is exciting. The ocean is unpredictable, and Barnaby and Basil have to leave.

2. The details show how much Basil loves the ocean. They also show why she will miss it.

3. They tell us that Basil is very tired and unhappy.

4. The last line shows us that Basil is finally happy enough to sleep.

Map Check 4

1. D
2. B
3. C
4. A
5. A
6. C
7. C
8. D
9. D
10. A
11. B
12. C

Mile 11: Plot, Setting, Character, Theme

Plot: Juan was grooming his pet cow, Henrietta, for the livestock competition at the county fair.

Theme: Juan knows that he's worked so hard that Henrietta will do well in the competition.

Setting: The story takes place in a barn at the fair. It is set in the present.

Characters: Juan is the main character. He is the boy who trained Henrietta. The girl with the braids is another character. She compliments Juan on his cow. Henrietta is Juan's cow that Juan raised since she was only six weeks old.

Mile 12: Getting Inside a Character's Head

1. Charaxos was drawn to Rhodopis. He feels that she is beautiful.

2. "Her beauty hypnotized Charaxos."

3. After Charaxos hears the tale of Rhodopis's childhood, Charaxos feels angry.

4. "Charaxos tightened his fists when he heard how she had been mistreated."

5. He feels happy for Rhodopis, but he is also sad because he is going to lose her.

6. "He paced back and forth in the garden. His stomach churned, and his heart seemed to be shriveling."

Generous	Angry	Sad
He buys her lots of things such as jewels and clothing. He builds her a house. He plants a garden for her. He works hard so that he can shower gifts on her.	"Charaxos tightened his fists when he heard how she had been mistreated."	His heart feels like it is shriveling. He has a lump in his throat.

Map Check 5

1. D
2. B
3. C
4. C
5. A
6. D
7. A
8. D
9. C
10. C
11. B
12. B

Mile 13: Metaphor, Simile, and Personification

1. **Simile:** a comparison between two different things that is formed with "like," "as," or "than"

2. **Metaphor:** a comparison between two things that is usually formed with a "to be" verb

3. **Personification:** a figure of speech that endows animals, ideas, or objects with human qualities and characteristics

1. Simile	6. Personification
2. Personification	7. Metaphor
3. Metaphor	8. Metaphor
4. Personification	9. Simile
5. Simile	10. Personification

Mile 14: Mood

1. Mysterious; simile: Underline "The old woman cackled like a hen . . . " or "The basement . . . smelled like a swamp."

2. Humorous or nonsensical; metaphor: Underline "Eliza Elizabeth was an elegant dandelion, a weed among women."

3. Serious; simile: Underline "The principal's face darkened suddenly like a storm sweeping across a sky."

4. Nonsensical; simile: Underline "Don't be as sharp as a butter knife."

5. Sorrowful; personification: Underline "He was hungry, and he wanted to go home" or "cast his sad eyes down toward the ground."

Mile 15: Elements and Poetry

The following words and terms should be matched

Rhyme: words that end with the same sounds

Mood: the way the poem makes you feel

Stanza: a grouping of two or more lines of poetry that are about the same length or share a rhyme scheme

Rhythm: the musical beat of the words

Theme: the author's meaning or the underlying moral

1. Two

2. Four

3. Two and three

4. Happy

5. Weather can't keep the author from feeling happy.

Map Check 6

1.	C	7.	D
2.	C	8.	C
3.	B	9.	A
4.	A	10.	D
5.	B	11.	B
6.	D	12.	D

Mile 16: Using Charts with Facts

1. 903

2. Chicago

3. 8:00 A.M.

4. 4:10 P.M.

5. Boston

Bollen Valley: At the midway point is a one-room schoolhouse that was used in the nineteenth century.

Cat's Meow: 6.5 Miles

Ann's Peak

Three Streams:

Mile 17: Using Charts with Stories

1. *An American Dictionary of the English Language*

2. A spelling book

3. more than hundred million

4. Contained standard ways of spelling and pronouncing words

Map Check 7

1. B
2. A
3. C
4. D
5. C
6. D
7. D
8. B

Ingredients

1. Bread
2. Mayonnaise
3. Cheese

Utensils

1. Cutting board
2. Knife

Steps

1. Take out two slices of bread.

2. Cut cheese into thin slices.

3. Spread mayonnaise on the bread.

4. Put the slices of cheese on the bread.

5. Put the bread together into a sandwich.

Mile 19: Reading Diagrams

1. Parentheses
2. Pictures
3. Written information
4. Icons
5. Labels

6. The title and introduction
7. Pluto
8. Venus and Mars
9. Jupiter
10. Venus

Map Check 8

1. C
2. C D
3. C
4. D
5. B
6. C

7. C
8. A
9. A
10. B
11. D
12. A

Mile 20: Looking Closely at the Text

1. Italics
2. Title
3. Asterisks
4. Subheadings

5. Parentheses
6. Quotation marks
7. Capital letters
8. Bold print

Mile 21: Making Comparisons

1. The ocean can be very dangerous.

2. Ocean weather can change quickly, turning a beautiful day into a stormy one.

3. Frightening   4. Chaotic

5. Personification is used when the author describes the clouds as "low and hairy in the skies / Like locks blown forward in the gleam of eyes." It makes the sky seem like an evil person.

6. Personification is used when the author says that "the sea opened its mouth, and we plunged into its salivating jaws . . . Then it spit us out roughly." This makes it seem like the sea is trying to devour the boat.

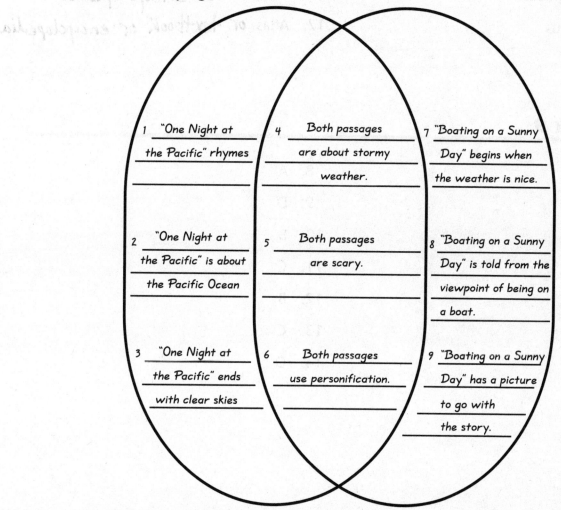

1. "One Night at the Pacific" rhymes

2. "One Night at the Pacific" is about the Pacific Ocean

3. "One Night at the Pacific" ends with clear skies

4. Both passages are about stormy weather.

5. Both passages are scary.

6. Both passages use personification.

7. "Boating on a Sunny Day" begins when the weather is nice.

8. "Boating on a Sunny Day" is told from the viewpoint of being on a boat.

9. "Boating on a Sunny Day" has a picture to go with the story.

Mile 22: Finding Out More

1. Textbook
2. Thesaurus
3. Dictionary
4. Almanac
5. Newspaper
6. Atlas
7. Encyclopedia
8. Thesaurus
9. Atlas
10. Dictionary
11. Almanac
12. Encyclopedia *or textbook*
13. Encyclopedia
14. Dictionary
15. Newspaper
16. Textbook *or encyclopedia*
17. Atlas *or textbook or encyclopedia*

Map Check 9

1. C
2. D
3. A
4. D
5. A
6. B
7. D
8. A
9. D
10. B
11. C
12. B
13. C
14. D

PRACTICE TEST 1 ANSWERS AND EXPLANATIONS

Answers and Explanations to End-of-Grade Reading Practice Test #1

1. **C** Reread the paragraph that describes Tankara's state of mind after he left his brother's house. It says his "mouth watered"; his brother was a "generous turtle"; and the string was "burning" his shell. Now look at the answer choices. Based on the description, you know that Tankara feels pained, (A), because of the string, thankful, (B), because his brother has given him salt, and hungry, (D), because his mouth is watering. There are no details to allow you to conclude that he's feeling bitter, (C). For this type of question, it's important to use Process of Elimination (POE).

2. **A** You know that Tankara took the lizard to court the second time because he wanted revenge, and he wanted to see what decision the elders would reach. You should reread the section in which Tankara discusses his reasoning to answer questions like this one. You know that (B) is incorrect because Tankara didn't want to go to court in the first place. (C) is also incorrect because Tankara doesn't know he'll be allowed to cut off the lizard's tail. (D) is incorrect because the salt has already been lost.

3. **D** To answer this type of question, reread the section that describes Tankara's revenge. You know that he claimed possession of the lizard, just as the lizard had claimed possession of his salt, because he sneaks up on the lizard and grabs him and declares that the lizard belonged to no one.

4. **A** You know that (A) is the correct answer because when Tankara goes to court he explains to the elders that he was dragging the salt because of his "tiny arms and legs." Using POE is a good way to answer this type of question. Read each answer choice and ask yourself, "Is there support for this in the story?" Eliminate the ones that are incorrect. You should be left with the correct answer. Even if you can only get rid of one or two answer choices, you'll have a better chance of guessing correctly.

5. **B** This is the correct answer because it's the only answer that is true. The author doesn't provide much description of the court elders, so (A) isn't correct. The story isn't about why turtles and lizards aren't friendly, so (C) isn't the right answer. It also doesn't tell why salt is important in cooking, so (D) can't be correct either. There are, however, several funny moments in the story.

6. **D** You can tell that Tankara felt "enraged but merciful" because the end of the story says that he was "filled with rage" but that his "heart softened," keeping him from killing the lizard. To answer these types of questions, it's important to reread part of the passage, looking for context clues. It's also important to make sure both adjectives describe the character or situation. Sometimes, one of the adjectives will be correct, like "revengeful" in (B), but the other one will not.

7. **D** Find the part of the passage where the word "abundant" is used and look for context clues. After it says that Tankara's salt stores were "abundant," it also says that his brother would "gladly share his wealth." Wealth implies that his brother has lots of salt. Therefore, his salt stores are "plentiful." If you didn't know the meaning of the word "plentiful," you could figure out the correct answer by using POE.

8. **A** You can tell this is the correct answer because the article says that "writing regularly is one of the keys to becoming a better writer." It also includes different exercises to help people learn to write regularly.

9. **C** Keeping lists and writing memories give writers instant subjects by "jumpstart[ing] the writing process." Go back and look at what the author says about the exercises. This will tell you why they're useful. You know that (A) and (B) aren't correct because the author doesn't mention anything about punctuation or dialogue. Making lists and writing memories surely wouldn't make a person *more* anxious about the writing process. If anything, a writer would feel *less* anxious after taking notes.

10. **C** It's important to read the questions carefully. This question is asking you which of the answer choices is not a reason for writing regularly. Therefore, you should eliminate the answer choices that are reasons for writing regularly. The passage mentions (A), (B), and (D). However, it doesn't say anything about writing a "best-selling novel."

11. **B** Again, it's important to read this question carefully because it's worded in the negative. It's asking you to decide which question is not answered by the passage. You can eliminate (A), (C), and (D) because they are all addressed. The article, however, doesn't say anything about the best time to write.

12. **D** Reread the quote from Natalie Goldberg, and then use POE. Does it define writer's block? No. Does it explain how to publish a book? No. Does it make the selection faster to read? No. Does it give authority to the selection because later it says that Goldberg has been teaching for twenty-five years? Yes!

13. **A** Look back at the examples. What purpose are they serving in the article? What purpose do examples generally serve? They usually show what others have done. The best way to answer this type of question is by using your critical thinking skills.

14. **C** You can tell that plastic wrap is not used as confetti material by looking at the list of things that can be used as confetti material. The best way to find a detail from the passage is to reread a section of the passage. Newspaper, (A), foil, (B), and tissue paper, (D), are all used to make confetti material.

15. **B** Find the part that explains how to decorate eggs. Which of the answer choices is mentioned? It says that you can use a "white crayon," but it doesn't mention any of the other answer choices. Therefore, you know that (B) must be the best answer choice.

16. **D** You know that (D) is correct because the directions say that the "bigger the hole, the easier it will be to remove the yolk and white from the egg." This implies that the purpose of the hole is to remove the contents of the egg. The best way to answer this type of question is to reread the section of the passage that mentions making the holes in the egg. None of the other answer choices really makes any sense.

17. **B** This question is asking you what's missing from the list of project materials. Are there any steps which require materials that aren't mentioned? The list mentions "stuff to decorate eggs," but it doesn't mention specific materials until the instructions. If you didn't read the instructions, you wouldn't know what materials you needed to decorate the eggs. That's why (B) is the correct answer choice.

18. **A** You know that making confetti is the second step because you do it right after decorating the eggs, which is the first step. To answer these types of questions, reread the directions, numbering each step. This will help you figure out their chronological order.

19. **C** To answer this question, use your critical thinking skills. What would you do if you were making cascarones, and you had read the directions once? You would gather the materials that you needed. Changing the order of the steps, (A), wouldn't help you! Neither would reading the instructions backward, (B), or memorizing them, (D).

20. **C** The theme is the underlying meaning of the poem. The way to answer this type of question is to read each answer choice and ask yourself whether it is supported by the poem. You know that the poem is about a force holding everything together because it says at the end of the poem that "there is one who holds this falling." The other answer choices do not give the theme of the poem.

21. **B** Reread the first four lines. Which of the final words rhyme? Lo rhymes with show, and wall rhymes with fall. Therefore, the first and second lines rhyme, and the third and fourth lines rhyme. That's all you need to do to answer this question!

22. **C** Mood refers to how the poem makes you feel. You know that the poem is playful because it describes a kitten chasing after leaves. The kitten is having fun, and it is fun to read the poem because it's such a light image.

23. **B** To answer this question, you should know the meaning of the word "theme." If you know that theme refers to a poem's underlying meaning, it's easy to choose answer (B). If you didn't know the definition of "theme," you could use POE to get rid of the silly choices like (A) and (D).

24. **C** To answer this question, you have to think about all of the reasons that an author might repeat the same word in a poem. Try to think about the symbolic meaning of the word. You know the author is not referring to the leaves that need to be raked because this is never mentioned in the poem. However, the poem is about different things ending; it does have a serious tone; and different objects do seem similar because the word "falling" is used to describe what happens to them.

25. **A** You know both poems share falling leaves because they both mention autumn and leaves falling from trees. All of the other answer choices are incorrect because they are either mentioned only in one of the poems or in neither. Always be sure to read the answer choices carefully!

26. **B** To answer this question, first find the word in the poem. Then use context clues to help you figure out its meaning. This question is slightly tricky because the context clues don't appear until much later in the poem. In line 18, it says the kitten "Crouches, stretches, paws, and darts," which are all words to suggest she is playing with the leaves.

27. **A** The best way to answer this type of question is first to summarize the description of autumn in each poem. In the first poem, the description is playful and fun. In the second poem, autumn seems to cause the destruction of many things. Now, look at each answer. Which one most resembles your descriptions of each poem? The first answer choice looks pretty good. Of course, always read every answer choice before making a final decision. (A) is still the best answer choice.

28. **B** You know that Serena's tennis career has been remarkable because the article says she is a "tennis sensation," and it describes how much she has improved since she began playing. You can eliminate the other choices because the article doesn't contain details to support them. Serena's tennis career certainly hasn't been ordinary!

29. **D** To answer this question reread the quote from Lyndrea to find out what it says about Serena's tennis career. The quote says that she took to tennis as soon as a racket was put in her hand. That proves that Serena had natural ability, making answer choice (D) correct. Her sister's comment doesn't support any of the other answer choices.

30. **A** Because Serena is a tennis star, it would make the most sense to visit a Web site on tennis stars to find out more about the way she trains. To answer research questions like this one, you need to be familiar with different types of reference materials and the type of information they supply. Just try to find the most reasonable answer choice. (D) is close, but (A) is the better answer choice.

31. **C** You have to understand the relationship between the boxes to answer graphic outline questions. This one tells you that the general subject is Serena, but it wants to know specific details about her at the U.S. Open. Your job is to fill in the missing detail about her at the U.S. Open. To find out what else she accomplished there, reread the section of the article on the U.S. Open. It says that she also matched Gibson's accomplishments, which is the correct answer. The other answer choices do not say what Serena did at the U.S. Open, so they wouldn't fit under the box titled, "U.S. Open."

32. **C** Serena Williams is a tennis sensation because she's so young and is a top-ranked tennis player. To answer this type of question, find the description in the passage and determine what reasons the author gives for generalizing. (A) is incorrect because losing a tournament is not a positive thing. Both (B) and (D) don't have anything to do with being sensational.

33. **C** Be sure to notice that this question is asking you about the things that the author did not do. To answer it, eliminate the things that the author did do. That means getting rid of (A), (B), and (D) because the author did all of these things. However, he never mentioned the animals he saw along the way. Therefore (C) is the correct answer choice.

34. **C** Reread the section on way stations. The passage describes the construction of the buildings (from "mud-colored bricks"), the facilities ("long, low huts"), and the selection of food (a "sack of flour," "coffee-pots," "a tin teapot," salt, and bacon). It doesn't, however, mention anything about parking. Therefore, you wouldn't be able to infer how parking at way stations or rest stops has changed.

35. **B** Twain traveled by stagecoach because it was faster than walking. You can learn this when he compares the progress his party made to the progress made by the emigrant wagon train. Twain never mentions riding a horse, (A), or his feelings about traveling with the mail, (C).

36. **B** This question is asking you to determine the differences between nineteenth-century and present-day travel. The first two items, stagecoaches and cars, are comparing two modes of travel. The second item in the "Present" box, gasoline, describes what powers cars. You have to decide what powers stagecoaches. (B), horses, is the best answer choice because they're what make stagecoaches move forward.

37. **D** You can tell that Mark Twain felt crowded in the stagecoach because the passage says that the coach was full of mailbags. In fact, there was so much mail that it almost touched their knees. The best way to answer a question about how the character feels is to reread part of the passage and look for context clues that will support a specific generalization. (A), (B), and (C) are incorrect because there are no clues in the first paragraph to support these generalizations.

38. **D** This question is asking you to decide which selection you would not read to find out more about stagecoaches. That means you should eliminate all of the choices that would be useful. Answer choices (A), (B), and (C) would be useful because they are all related to stagecoaches or the period of time during which stagecoaches were used. Answer choice (D) would not be useful because it's too general. It could be about any aspect of the postal service during any time period.

39. **A**   Asking about the "best reason" to read a story is another way of asking about the main idea. Often, you can find the answers to these types of questions by rereading the introduction or first paragraph. The introduction to this story says it's about Mark Twain's trip by stagecoach, which makes (A) the best answer choice. Both (C) and (D) describe specific details from the story, not the main idea. (B) is incorrect because there's little information about how pioneers live.

40. **A**   An autobiography is a story told from a real person's point of view, and the word "I" is often used. Because this is a personal account of Mark Twain's journey by stagecoach, you know that it's an autobiography. The other answer choices don't describe the essential characteristics of an autobiography. For example, details and humor could be present in a fictional story as well as an autobiography.

41. **D**   Each of the parentheses contains examples of everyday objects that represent different kinds of matter. You know that (A), (B), and (C) are incorrect because the information in the parentheses doesn't fulfill the function described. The parentheses don't offer scientific terms, and they don't explain how matter changes states. And while the parentheses may make may the passage slightly longer, that isn't their function or purpose.

42. **B**   The section on gases says that gases have the "most energy." To answer questions about details, reread the section where you're most likely to find the answer. This is a simple fact question, and you can always answer these types of questions by reading carefully.

43. **B**   You can tell that the pictures are supposed to give examples from everyday life because each one shows a different state of matter. The best way to answer this type of question is to use common sense and look at how the element is being used. The pictures have nothing to do with how quickly you can read the passage (A), and (C) and (D) only describe one specific picture—not the purpose of all of them.

44. **D**   You know finding a Web site on science would be the best way to find out more information because matter is a scientific subject. For research questions, ask yourself where you would first look if you were in a library. Usually your common sense will lead you to the correct answer. Would buying a helium balloon tell you more about all three states of matter? Nope, so (A) is wrong. Would reading an article about snow tell you more about all three states of matter? Not really, so (B) is wrong. Boiling a pot of water might show you how liquid changes to gas, but it won't tell you about solids. (D) is clearly the best choice.

45. **C** The first way to find the meaning of a word is always to look for clues in the passage. Often, if you carefully read the whole section where the word appears, you'll get a better idea of what the word means. This is always what you should do first, before asking someone to tell you the definition or looking in a reference book.

46. **A** You know that (A) is the correct answer because Cleary says that she writes books that she would have liked when she was a child. The best approach for answering this question is to skim the article, looking for the part that describes Cleary's motivation for writing children's books. Neither (B) nor (C) is mentioned as a reason that Cleary writes, even though she has sold many books, and her husband did suggest the idea for her first book. (D) doesn't describe anything stated in the article.

47. **D** Cleary went from being a non-reader as a child to one of America's best-selling authors as an adult. That's why (D) is the best answer choice. Remember that theme questions are asking you what you learned from the passage. You can eliminate (A) because the passage says reading can be fun. (B) and (C) aren't correct either because the passage doesn't deal with these as main topics.

48. **B** You know that Cleary felt frustrated and bored because the passage says she "tried to guess the meaning" of the words and the sentences she read "put her to sleep." To answer questions about a character's feelings, make sure you go back to the passage and look for clues in the character's actions and expressions. Both (A) and (C) are partially correct; Cleary felt both "anxious" and "nervous" about reading, but she didn't feel either "intrigued" or "gifted."

49. **A** To answer this question, you have to figure out what the author did not write about. The author of the article mentions (B), (C), and (D). The author does not mention (A). Make sure you check your answers by reviewing the passage.

50. **D** Reading *The Dutch Twins* was Cleary's first enjoyable reading experience. How do you know this? Because the passage says that Cleary was surprised to find that she enjoyed the book. To answer questions about a character's motivation, reread the section of the passage that talks about the change in the character's attitude. In this case, Cleary's attitude toward reading changes in the fifth paragraph.

51. **D** It may help to answer this question by using POE. Read each answer choice and ask yourself whether it is something you would learn by reading the quote. The quote provides most support for the idea that Cleary remembered what it was like to be a child because she could still remember the kinds of books that she liked to read. It doesn't explain anything about the difficulty of finding a good book or about how good she was at helping children pick out books.

52. **C** Ask yourself what you learned from reading this passage. Then read the answer choices. Which thing did you not learn? It's clear that (C) is correct because the passage doesn't provide information on how to tell children how to write best-selling children's books. It could encourage children not to give up easily, so (A) and (B) aren't right. It could also inspire children to read more, so (D) is also not right.

53. **B** The best way to answer questions about the author's attitude is by using POE. It's clear from the tone of the passage that the author feels neither furious, (C), nor disrespectful, (D). Now, look at the remaining answer choices. Is the author bored or intrigued. Reread the opening paragraph. It says that it's difficult to believe that Beverly Cleary was once such a poor reader. You know from this that the author is curious or intrigued by Cleary. The author is not bored at all.

54. **D** Reading the title and introduction is always the best thing to do before reading the entire passage. On the North Carolina EOG Test in Reading, this will always be the best answer.

55. **D** Quotes are usually used to signify that something is being said by someone. That means you should focus on answer choices (A) and (D). Then you have to decide whether the quote belongs to Hoyle or Witcombe. By looking at the final paragraph, you can tell that the quote is from Witcombe, who was called a Stonehenge expert earlier in the passage.

56. **B** Magazines are usually published on a regular basis, and they would likely contain the most up-to-date information of the answer choices given. Although both a travel book, (A), and an encyclopedia, (C), might contain information about Stonehenge, it wouldn't be as recent as a magazine. A dictionary, (D), wouldn't help you at all.

57. **C** The passage says that the burial mounds surrounding Stonehenge suggest that it was used as a religious temple. The best way to answer a detail question is to skim the passage for key words in the question like "religious temple." All of the other answer choices provide evidence of other theories about Stonehenge. Only answer choice (B) answers the question at hand.

58. **C** You can tell that (C) supports the idea that Stonehenge arouses curiosity because the phrase contains the word "puzzle." That is another word for "arouses curiosity." To answer these kinds of questions, you need to read each answer choice and decide which one seems the most similar to the idea suggested in the question.

59. **A** To answer questions about how you could use the passage, you need to decide what the passage is mainly about. In this case, it's about Stonehenge, a mysterious structure. Now look at the answer choices. You know the answer is (A) because Stonehenge is an example of an architectural mystery. (B), (C), and (D) are too general and are only distantly related to the subject matter.

60. **C** To answer this question, you need to figure out what the story is mainly about. Because the three family members puzzle over the combination to the lock and finally figure it out, (C) seems to be the best answer. You might get tripped up by (D), but keep in mind that the point of the story is to show a normal family. It's to show how a family tries to solve a problem.

61. **D** Reread the section that describes the family figuring out the forgotten combination. You can tell that (D) is the correct answer because the family members discuss the kinds of mistakes that the father usually makes. (C) does not accurately describe what happens in the story. The family works together to figure out the forgotten combination.

62. **A** You know that the forgetful father was born in 1942 because Scott asks his mother the date of his father's birth. To answer questions about details, you must reread part of the passage to find the answer. Don't expect to memorize all of the information in the passage. Once you know the kind of information you're looking for, you can always go back and look for it.

63. **B** The moral of the story is what you learn from the story. This family solved a problem by working together. You know this because they didn't figure out the combination until they all sat down together. So the story is trying to say that working together can be more helpful than working alone.

64. **D** To answer this question, you must decide which answer choice does not refer to the ocean or a body of water. (A) contains seagulls, which are sea birds. (B) refers to an island. (C) refers to the ocean. Therefore, you know that (D) is the correct answer. It doesn't give any clues that the story takes place near the ocean. If you only read the statement in (D), you might think the story took place in Kansas!

65. **A** To answer vocabulary questions, always go back and find the word in the passage. In this case, you have to decide how you figured out the meaning of the word. You can eliminate (B) and (C) immediately because the passage doesn't have either a glossary or an illustration. You know that the author gives context clues because she uses the word marina and then describes boats coming and going.

PRACTICE TEST 2
ANSWERS AND
EXPLANATIONS

ANSWERS AND EXPLANATIONS TO END-OF-GRADE READING PRACTICE TEST #2

1. **D** You know the author wants you to feel impressed because she mentions that Molly has been inventing things since she was three, a very young age. To answer questions about the author's attitude, you should look closely at the kinds of words the author uses to describe a person or a situation. Both (B) and (C) are incorrect because there's nothing irritating or amusing about what the author says about Molly. The author certainly doesn't want you to feel confused by Molly, (A), so (D) is the best answer choice.

2. **C** "Old hand" is an example of figurative language. If you don't know the meaning of the phrase, you should reread the second paragraph. Look for context clues nearby. After the author calls Molly an "old hand" at inventing, you find out that Molly has been inventing things since she was young. There's your answer!

3. **B** You know that Molly is creative because the first paragraph says that she often uses her imagination to solve problems. To answer questions about character or people, look for clues in the passage. Also ask yourself how you feel about the person once you've finished reading the passage. There is no reason to believe that she is greedy, (A), or insecure, (D). She might be sophisticated, (C), but creative is a much better description of her.

4. **C** To answer web questions, you have to determine the relationship between the different boxes. For this question, the question mark describes all of the different things—Lizard Snout, Carbonated Drink Squirt Stopper, and Straw Sinker—that Molly has invented. What do these items have in common? You know that they're all inventions.

5. **A** From the passage, you know that Molly is an inventor, but you don't necessarily know that she's a genius, so (D) isn't the right choice. You can also eliminate answer choices (B) and (C) because they don't have anything to do with the passage. If you wanted to find out more about Molly, you'd read a book about recent inventions.

6. **D** This is an easy question. The first thing you should always do before jumping in to the selection is read the title, introduction, and first paragraph and try to identify the main idea. Whenever you're asked this question, the answer will be the same.

7. **C** Don't be tricked by the way this question is worded. You have to decide which answer choice is evidence that the objects seen were not UFOs. The meteor sighting is the correct answer, because the passage says that experts think the pilots could have mistaken the meteor for a UFO. The best way to answer a detail question is to use Process of Elimination (POE). Read each answer choice, and return to the passage to see how the information is being used.

8. **C** You know that Arnold saw the first UFO because the second paragraph says that the Roswell incident was the first UFO sighting. The best way to answer detail questions is to refer back to the passage. Don't try to memorize all of the information in the passage. Find out what the question is asking and skim the passage to find the answer.

9. **D** Long quotes are always indented. Even if you didn't know this, you could use POE to figure out the correct answer. The selection doesn't say anything about speeches, so (A) isn't the right answer choice. While the indented paragraph argues that UFOs don't exist, this is not the reason it's indented, (B). There's also nothing to indicate that it's the most important part of the passage, (C). Right before the indented part, the passage says, "Sagan continued." This is what tells you it's a continuation of a quote from Sagan.

10. **C** You could find current information on UFOs in a book, because some books are written specifically about UFOs. A magazine from 1947, (A), would not have current information about UFOs. An almanac, (B), and a dictionary, (D), are both reference books that would have very little current information about UFOs.

11. **A** Use your common sense to answer this question. Because you know the passage is about UFOs, the most related topic is on the mysteries of space. The history of airplanes, (B), has nothing to do with UFOs. Answer choices (C) and (D) are both too general. (A) is the best answer choice.

12. **B** The best way to answer this question is to use Process of Elimination. Get rid of all of the answer choices that are addressed in the passage. Storing lettuce, (A), is addressed in the first tip on how to begin cooking, so (A) isn't correct. Cooking's creativity, (C), is addressed in the section on the ways chefs invent new recipes, so (C) isn't correct either. You know that (D) is incorrect too because the importance of preparing foods simply is addressed in the tip entitled "Stay Simple." The passage mentions that Chin teaches about the difference between paprika and chili powder, but it doesn't actually tell the difference between the two. (B) is the best answer choice.

13. **C** Again, don't be deceived by the way this question is worded. Your job is to figure out which answer choice is not mentioned as a reason to learn to cook. Read each answer choice and return to the passage to see whether it's mentioned. By doing this, you'll realize that earning a lot of money as a chef is never mentioned.

14. **A** The author included two tips to help readers become better cooks. You know this because the author says that the tips will "help you begin cooking." (B) is incorrect because earlier in the article the author says that chefs attend professional cooking schools. (C) has nothing to do with the author's reasons, and (D) is more of a tip than a reason for including the tips.

15. **C** Buying fresh ingredients and staying simple help cooks recognize the natural goodness of food. You know this because the author says this in each of the tips for getting started in the kitchen. To answer questions like this one, always skim the passage to find the answer. Then read carefully and you should have no problem finding the right answer.

16. **A** Always use POE to answer main idea questions. Eating in good restaurants, (B), is not mentioned in the article. The author says that anyone can learn the basics without becoming a chef, (C). The author also says that being creative allows you to cook without recipes. That leaves you with answer choice (A), which is the best possible choice.

17. **D** The author interviewed Chin to provide comments from an expert. You know Chin is an expert because the article says she has run her own restaurant and taught cooking lessons. Quotes are generally used to lend authority to an article, rather than to impress the reader, (A). Because Chin doesn't talk about becoming a professional chef, you know that (B) is incorrect.

18. **D** Because this question is asking about the use of parentheses in the second point, what should you do first? Go look at the parenthesis again! Hopefully you can tell that the purpose is to offer a scientific term. A molecule is the scientific word for particles of matter. If you weren't sure about this one, use POE to help you. Does it give the Latin word or provide an abbreviation? No, "molecule" doesn't seem like it's in Latin, and it's not any shorter than "matter." So, right away, you can get rid of (A) and (B).

19. **B** You should know that sound depends on particles of matter because Step 2 says exactly this. To answer a question about a detail, always return to the diagram and read the part that you think will be most relevant. Vocal cords can make noises, but noises don't depend on them, so (C) is wrong. Likewise, noise can travel through air, but it can also travel through liquids such as water, so (D) is wrong too. (A) doesn't make much sense at all.

20. **B** Look at the picture and try to figure out what it's good for. Hopefully you can tell that its purpose is to show how sound travels. It doesn't necessarily make the picture faster to read, (A), and it doesn't give any information about either the speed or density of sound waves, (C) or (D).

21. **D** Use common sense and critical thinking to answer questions about where you would find more information about certain subjects. Listening, (A), reading about music, (B), and going to a rock concert, (C), all have something to do with hearing and music, but they're not directly related to information on sound. A scientific article on hearing is most related to sound because it explores how you receive sound. Therefore, (D) is actually the best answer choice.

22. **C** On the North Carolina EOG Test in Reading, you're expected first to look for context clues in the passage to figure out the definition of an unfamiliar word. That means if you didn't understand the definition of the word "vibrating," you should see if the word was defined within the text. If you still can't figure it out, then you can use a dictionary or ask an adult for its meaning.

23. **A** Meng Chaing-nu throws herself into the river because she doesn't want to marry the emperor. It says almost exactly this in the story. To answer questions about character's motivation, always reread the section that describes the action you are being asked about. Both (B) and (C) describe what happens after Meng Chaing-nu throws herself into the river, so they're not correct. (D) describes what happens just before she jumps into the river.

24. **C** By rereading the section on Meng Chiang-nu's journey, you can determine how she feels. It says she is "overcome with fatigue" and that she "cursed the emperor" who had taken her husband away. She also "became quite lost" at one point. All of these details show that Meng Chiang-nu feels angry, exhausted, and lost. They don't suggest that she feels optimistic. That's why the correct answer is (C).

25. **D** Meng Chiang-nu tricks the emperor to have her husband buried properly because she agrees to marry him, even though she never intends to do so. To answer questions about a character's actions, reread the section about the incident in question. (A), (B), and (C) are incorrect because they explain how Meng Chiang-nu takes other actions in the story, but not how she has her husband buried properly. Only (D) addresses this particular question.

26. **A** Wan Hsi-liang is ordered by the emperor to leave his wife. You know this because the first paragraph of the story says that emperor orders his servants to leave their homes and build the wall. Always reread the part of the passage most relevant to the question to answer questions about a character's motivation.

27. **D** The best way to answer questions about characters' feelings is to reread the part of the passage connected to the question and look for context clues. After the wall falls, it says that the people are "awestruck," and in their hearts, they "harbored secret gladness." The choice that describes these feelings is (D). "Shocked" is another word for "awestruck," and "happy" is a synonym for "gladness." None of the other answer choices gives a better description of the feelings of the people after the wall crumbles.

28. **B** Use common sense to draw conclusions about the author's choices. By reading the answer choices, you can decide how the author makes the story surprising. You know that (A) and (D) are incorrect because neither is described in much detail. (C) is also wrong because merely describing Meng Chiang-nu's journey isn't especially surprising. It is surprising when we learned that Meng Chiang-nu has magical powers.

29. **D** In the paragraph in which Meng Chiang-nu is "consumed with apprehension," it also says that her sadness grows. You can use this clue to conclude that Meng Chiang-nu is worried. This tells you her feelings didn't have to do with hunger, (A). She also wasn't either understanding, (B), or calm, (C). Remember that the best way to answer a vocabulary question is to reread the section in which the word or phrase appears and look for context clues.

30. **B** Think about your overall impression of Clemente. Knowing that he worked hard to become a baseball player and always tried to help others, how would you characterize him? (B) is the best answer because it describes Clemente's road to professional baseball and his contributions to Puerto Rico. In answer choice (A), one of the adjectives is accurate. There is nothing in the passage that tells you that Clemente is strange or tired so (C) and (D) are wrong too. It's always important to read both of the adjectives carefully.

31. **A** Clemente mentored other Hispanic baseball players. The article says that he took other Hispanic players under his wing and offered baseball clinics throughout Puerto Rico. Always return to the passage to answer questions about details. Once you know what you're looking for, you can usually quickly find the correct information. If you read the passage carefully, you should have been able to get rid of (B) and (C) because they're not true at all. (D) is true, but it doesn't answer the question.

32. **D** You know from reading the article that Clemente was deeply committed to Puerto Rico. When you're answering questions about people or characters, you can base your general impression on the character's actions and author's descriptions of the character. The sentence in the question doesn't tell about Clemente's attitude toward his success; it merely says that success didn't erase his past. Plus, Clemente certainly isn't arrogant—he was humble—so (C) can't be the correct answer choice. (D) is the best answer choice.

33. **C** Because the question is worded in the negative, you're looking for the reason that you would not read about Clemente. To answer this question, first eliminate all of the reasons you would read about him. The article discusses Clemente's respect for his family and community, (A), his hard work, (B), and his desire to use his gifts to help others, (D). You probably wouldn't read the article to develop a strong throwing arm because the article doesn't provide information about how to do this. Therefore, (C) is the best answer choice.

34. **D** You know that Clemente was an expert "spray hitter" because the article says so. Always go back and reread part of the passage to answer detail questions. You will have enough time on the test to find the correct answer.

35. **B** The author wants to make you feel respectful of Clemente. This is because of the kind of language that the author uses throughout the passage to describe the baseball player. The author calls him "great," tells how he spent "many hours" perfecting his baseball skills, and describes all of the good deeds he did in Puerto Rico. Because the author's tone is positive and admiring, you feel respectful rather than sad, offended, or confused.

36. **A** Answer this question by using POE. Get rid of each fact that appears in the passage. The fact that doesn't appear in the passage is the amount of Clemente's salary when he played for Pittsburgh. Therefore, that's the correct answer.

37. **D** Keep in mind that the main idea describes the passage as a whole, not just parts of it. The North Carolina EOG Test in Reading will sometimes try to trick you by using details from the passage as answer choices. Both (A) and (B), for example, describe different aspects of the article, but not the main idea. In contrast, answer choice (C) has nothing to do the piece. The best answer choice is (D) because it describes how Clemente tried to live.

38. **C** You know the "City Night" is about the energy of cities because the poet describes the city's twenty-four hour day and exclaims, "hurray!" This shows that the poet is excited about the energy. Asking about the meaning of a poem is another way of asking about its main idea. Think about the meaning of the poem and how it makes you feel. In this case, the meaning isn't about gazing out windows, artists selling their work, or getting used to a city's noise.

39. **C** Look at the words that are used in "A London Thoroughfare, 2 A.M." They include words like "glare," "slow-moving," "squalid," "sinister," and "alien." They are gloomy words, and the poet's obsession with how the moon cannot light the city indicates that she is feeling pessimistic. Gloomy is the word which best describes the tone of this poem. To answer questions about tone, always look at the kinds of words the poet or author uses, and think about how they make you feel.

40. **B** These kinds of questions should be easy for you. The first line rhymes with the third line because "by" rhymes with "sky." That's all there is to this question.

41. **B** We know "squalid' is a tough word. But if you look for the word in context, you'll see that the poet is describing a sad scene of tramps dozing in the streets, nightwalkers passing by, and a sinister city. The poet's description is very negative, which allows you to eliminate (A) and (C) which are both positive. There's also no evidence of the city being confusing. You can infer that the word "squalid" means "miserable," which is answer choice (B).

42. **C** Alive is not repeated to explain why the speaker is still awake. You know this because the poem never focuses on the speaker of the poem. The speaker describes the liveliness of the city and how the city makes her feel alive, but she never mentions why she's awake. Use POE to figure this out, if you need to.

43. **B** Use common sense to answer this question. Because poetry is sometimes more difficult to read than prose, it's a good idea to read slowly and make sure you understand each line. Ignoring figurative language, (A), reading lines forward and backward, (C), or guessing the meaning, (D), won't help you truly understand a poem. To read a poem for meaning, it helps to read slowly and summarize the meaning at the end of each line, (B).

44. **A** Make a list of the major elements in each poem. When you're finished, compare your lists and see what both poems share. In this case, you know that both poems are about cities. All of the other answer choices are contained in one poem, but not the other. For example, only "City Night" describes people walking their dogs, so (D) can't be right.

45. **B** The moon in the first poem is losing its battle with the city, because the poem says that "she cannot light the city." It shows that the city is aggressive and unnatural. In the other poem, "City Night," the moon is bright enough to light up all of the activity.

46. **B** Listing the paste ingredients under "Materials" would make the craft project easier. Without listing the paste ingredients under "Materials," you might not realize you needed these ingredients. Larger print size wouldn't really make the craft project easier to do, so (A) isn't correct. And it might be nice to know about the history of masks—or see a picture of one—but it also wouldn't make the project easier. (B) is the best answer choice.

47. **D** Find the step that describes placing the newspaper behind the tinfoil mold. This is where the directions will explain the purpose of doing it. When you're answering detail questions, always go back and find the information in the passage. There's no reason to try to memorize everything the first time you read it. Newspaper is placed behind the tinfoil mold to prevent the mold from being damaged.

48. **B** The directions say that once the papier mâché has dried, you can paint your mask. That's why you know that you can use paint to decorate a mask. Both the newspaper, (A), and tinfoil, (D), are used for other purposes. Makeup, (C), is never mentioned. (B) is clearly the best answer choice.

49. **C** This question is easy. Just scan the list of materials and the paste instructions to see which of the answer choices is not mentioned. After you've done this, you know that glue is not needed for this project. Newspaper, (A), flour, (B), and tinfoil, (D), are all mentioned.

50. **A** This question is asking you to determine which answer choice is the first step in making a mask. Read through the answer choices to see which comes first. The directions tell you that preparing the paper for the papier mâché, (C), painting the mask, (B), and allowing the mask to dry, (D), all come after you have made the mold of your face. That's why (A) is the best answer choice.

51. **C** Use your common sense to answer this question. The best way to read instructions is to read them quickly at first, and then read each step carefully just before you begin it. If you don't read through the entire set of directions initially, you might reach a point where you're confused or don't have the correct materials. You certainly don't need to memorize every step, (B), or read every other step, (D).

52. **D** Hector Henry doesn't clean his room because he thinks there's a ghost in the house, he "collapses on the couch," and stops everything. The best way to answer questions about a character's motivation is to reread the passage looking for clues in things the characters say and ways that they behave. Then look at the answer choices to see which fits. Hector became too terrified to clean his room, so (D) is the best answer choice.

53. **A** Read the passage again if you weren't sure of this answer. Ziad proposed calling the police. You know this because he suggests to Hector Henry that they call the police. None of the other people are mentioned when Ziad proposes calling someone. You can even use POE to get rid of (B), (C), and (D).

54. **C** To answer questions about an author's motivations, think about how the story affected you. Did it make you laugh? Did it make you scared? Because you find out at the end of the story that the ghost is just a curtain, this is a pretty funny story. Therefore, you know the author wrote it to entertain you.

55. **A** The author defines mementos in the parentheses immediately following the word. Always find the vocabulary word in the passage to decide how the author is revealing its meaning. Because the author doesn't use italics or footnotes, you can use the POE to get rid of (C) and (D) right away.

56. **B** You know that Hector Henry is paralyzed with fear after he sees the ghost. This is because he collapses on the couch, unable to do anything except wait for his parents to return home. Reread the part of the story after Hector Henry sees the ghost. Make sure to look for context clues to answer these kinds of questions.

57. **C** To answer this question, all you have to do is read the quotes and decide which ones are scary and which ones aren't. You have to find the answer choice that doesn't show how scared Hector Henry is. Answer choices (A), (B), and (D) describe some aspect of Hector Henry's fear. However, answer choice (C) does not. Although the ladder is creaky, you don't learn anything about how Hector Henry is feeling.

58. **B** The author's family collects water in rain barrels because the well water is limited. From this, you can draw a conclusion that the well water might run out. You can learn that the other answer choices are incorrect by rereading the section about the well. It doesn't mention anything about whether the water is clean, their thirst, or it being their only source of water. That means (A), (C), and (D) aren't right, leaving only (B) as the right answer.

59. **D** The author feels special about living on an island. You can tell that she feels this way because she calls it a "unique" experience in the second paragraph and gives many examples of the ways that it is unique. You can eliminate normal, (A), because the author often describes how it's different from the way that most people live. You can also eliminate envious, (B), and angry, (C), because there are no context clues to suggest the author feels envious or angry.

60. **B** To complete graphic organizers, you have to figure out what's being compared. In this case, it's life on an island versus mainland life. You know that the missing item is water from a well, (B), because the other box says water from a faucet. On the mainland, people get water from a faucet. On the island in the story, however, the people obtain water from a well.

61. **A** Autobiographical stories are told from one person's perspective and usually use the word, "I." To answer questions about literary forms, you simply need to know the meaning of words like "autobiography." Unusual circumstances, (B), or stories about contemporary life, (C), could occur in almost any kind of book. And fictional events, (D), certainly don't exist in a nonfiction source such as an autobiography.

62. **C** There are many differences between living on the mainland and living on an island. However, you are supposed to find the answer choice that is not different. For example, you know that communication is different. How? Because the family on the island doesn't even have a phone. So (A) isn't right. Also, the family has to take a boat for transportation and for grocery shopping, so that's pretty different! Friendships, (C), is the correct answer because having friends is the same on an island as it is on the mainland. Make sure you always read the questions carefully. In this case, you should eliminate the answer choices that are differences from mainland living.

63. **D** You can answer this question using common sense. You know that a cookbook filled with seafood recipes would probably not be very helpful if you wanted to find more information about living on an island. The reference book on island communities, (A), would definitely include information about living on islands. The tale about being shipwrecked on an island, (B), or growing up on an island, (C), are both directly related to living on an island.

64. **A**   Asking about the purpose of reading something is another way of asking about the main idea. You know that this passage is mainly about how life is different on an island. The other answer choices describe different elements of living on an island, but they're too specific to summarize the overarching point. Answer choice (A) is closest to the theme of the passage.

65. **C**   Look for a method that the author did not use make the passage fun to read. You know that the author didn't make the passage fun to read by describing the lakes and rivers of the island because the island doesn't have any lakes or rivers! Always use POE to answer these kinds of questions. Read each answer choice, check the passage to see if the information is included, and then eliminate it if it's included.

Cool Books for Cool Readers

The more you read, the better you get at it. But reading stories, novels, and poetry will help you do much more than improve in school. You can read for fun and to escape into fantasy. You can also find out about the lives of children like yourself who have grown up in places, cultures, or time periods different from your own. It's just like going on a trip, except that you don't have to worry about the driving!

The following list includes books recommended by teachers, librarians, and—most importantly—other children. Check out the books in your library, and take home the ones that seem interesting to you. If you like a book, you can ask your parents, friends, teacher, or librarian to recommend others like it. If you like a book, but it's too hard for you, ask a parent to read it to you. But if you're not hooked after you've read a few chapters of a book, don't worry about it. Try something else. Nobody's grading you! Enjoy!

Babbitt, Natalie. *Tuck Everlasting.* (Fantasy)

Baum, L. Frank. *The Wizard of Oz.* (Fantasy)

Blume, Judy. *Just as Long as We're Together.* (Contemporary Fiction)

> *Here's to You, Rachel Robinson* is the sequel to this book. Blume has written many other popular books for young people, including *Tales of a Fourth Grade Nothing,* the first in a series about Peter Hatcher and his little brother, Fudge.

Burnett, Frances Hodgson. *The Secret Garden.* (Classic)

Carroll, Lewis. *Alice's Adventures in Wonderland.* (Classic)

> Alice's adventures continue in *Through the Looking Glass.*

Cleary, Beverly. *Beezus and Ramona.* (Contemporary Fiction)

> This book begins Cleary's series about Ramona Quimby. This story is told from the point of view of Ramona's older sister, Beezus.

Dahl, Roald. *James and the Giant Peach.* (Fantasy)

Other favorite books by Dahl include *Charlie and the Chocolate Factory, Matilda,* and *Fantastic Mr. Fox.*

Danziger, Paula. *The Cat Ate My Gymsuit.* (Contemporary Fiction)

Also try Danziger's series about Amber Brown, which begins with *Amber Brown is Not a Crayon.*

Dorris, Michael. *Guests.* (Contemporary Fiction)

Erdrich, Louise. *The Birchbark House.* (Historical Fiction)

Farley, Walter. *The Black Stallion.* (Classic)

The Black Stallion Returns is the next book in Farley's series about the magnificent stallion, Black.

Fitzhugh, Louise. *Harriet the Spy.* (Contemporary Fiction)

Fleischman, Paul. *Seedfolks.* (Contemporary Fiction)

Gipson, Fred. *Old Yeller.* (Classic)

Grahame, Kenneth. *The Wind in the Willows.* (Classic)

Konigsburg, E. L. *From the Mixed-Up Files of Mrs. Basil E. Frankweiler.* (Contemporary Fiction)

L'Engle, Madeleine. *A Wrinkle in Time.* (Science Fiction, Contemporary Fiction)

L'Engle's series about the Murry family continues in *A Swiftly Tilting Planet, A Wind in the Door,* and *Many Waters.* Also try *A Ring of Endless Light,* a favorite in her series about Vicky Austin and her family.

Lewis, C. S. *The Lion, the Witch, and the Wardrobe.* (Classic, Fantasy)

The first book written in the *Chronicles of Narnia.*

King-Smith, Dick. *Babe, the Gallant Pig.* (Fantasy)

Lowry, Lois. *Number the Stars.* (Historical Fiction)

Mead, Alice. *Junebug.* (Contemporary Fiction)

Myers, Walter Dean. *Me, Mop, and the Moondance Kid.* (Contemporary Fiction)

MacLachlan, Patricia. *Sarah, Plain and Tall.* (Historical Fiction)

Namioka, Lensey. *Yang the Youngest and His Terrible Ear.* (Contemporary Fiction)

Norton, Mary. *The Borrowers.* (Fantasy)

O'Brien, Robert C. *Mrs. Frisby and the Rats of NIMH.* (Fantasy)

O'Dell, Scott. *Island of the Blue Dolphins.* (Historical Fiction)

Pullman, Philip. *The Firework-Maker's Daughter.* (Fantasy)

> For a worthwhile challenge, try Pullman's fantasy *The Golden Compass* and its sequel, *The Subtle Knife.*

Paterson, Katherine. *Bridge to Terabithia.* (Contemporary Fiction)

> Other popular books by Paterson include *The Great Gilly Hopkins, The Master Puppeteer,* and *The King's Equal,* an original fairy tale.

Rowling, J. K. *Harry Potter and the Sorcerer's Stone.* (Fantasy)

> The first book in a wildly popular series that includes *Harry Potter and the Chamber of Secrets, Harry Potter and the Prisoner of Azkaban,* and *Harry Potter and the Goblet of Fire.*

de Saint-Exupery, Antoine. *The Little Prince.* (Classic)

Scieszka, Jon. *Summer Reading Is Killing Me!* (Fantasy)

> Scieszka has written many other funny books for children. Try *The Stinky Cheese Man and Other Fairly Stupid Tales* and *Knights of the Kitchen Table.*

Selden, George. *The Cricket in Times Square.* (Classic)

Silverstein, Shel. *Where the Sidewalk Ends.* (Poetry)

> Silverstein has written two other books of funny poetry: *A Light in the Attic and Falling Up.*

Sobol, Donald. *Encyclopedia Brown and the Case of the Slippery Salamander.* (Contemporary Fiction)

> This book is one of the latest in a series of stories about Encyclopedia Brown. You can try to solve each mystery on your own. Then, you can find the solution in the back of the book.

Soto, Gary. *The Skirt.* (Contemporary Fiction)

> Soto has written many other books, including *Baseball in April and Other Stories* and *Crazy Weekend. Summer on Wheels* is the sequel to Crazy Weekend.

Speare, Elizabeth George. *The Sign of the Beaver.* (Historical Fiction)

> Also try Speare's classic, *The Witch of Blackbird Pond.*

Stolz, Mary. *Go Fish.* (Fiction)

White, E. B. *Charlotte's Web.* (Classic)

Also try White's other books for children: *Stuart Little and The Trumpet of the Swan.*

Wilder, Laura Ingalls. *Little House in the Big Woods.* (Classic, Historical Fiction)

This book is the first in Wilder's series about her life as a pioneer girl. The second book in the series is *Little House on the Prairie.*

Yep, Laurence. *Ribbons.* (Contemporary Fiction)

The Cook's Family is the sequel to this book.

If students need to know it, it's in our Roadmap Guides!

Roadmap to 3rd Grade Math, North Carolina Edition
0-375-75580-2 • $14.95

Roadmap to 3rd Grade Reading, North Carolina Edition
0-375-75577-2 • $14.95

Roadmap to 5th Grade Math, North Carolina Edition
0-375-75581-0 • $14.95

Roadmap to 5th Grade Reading, North Carolina Edition
0-375-75578-0 • $14.95

Roadmap to 8th Grade Math, North Carolina Edition
0-375-75582-9 • $14.95

Roadmap to 8th Grade Reading, North Carolina Edition
0-375-75579-9 • $14.95

 The Princeton Review — Available at your local bookstore